Frommer's®

24 GREAT walks in CHICAGO

WILEY

Wiley Publishing, Inc.

Author: Max Grinnell
Managing Editor: Apostrophe S Limited
Series Editor: Donna Wood
Art Editor: Alison Fenton
Page Layout: Andrew Milne
Copy Editor: Jackie Staddon
Proofreader: Edith Summerhayes
Picture Researcher: Vivien Little
Production: Stephanie Allen
Image retouching and internal repro: Sarah Montgomery

Edited, designed and produced by AA Publishing.
© Automobile Association Developments Limited 2009

Published by AA Publishing.

Published in the United States by
Wiley Publishing, Inc.
111 River Street, Hoboken, NJ 07030

Find us online at Frommers.com

Frommer's is a registered trademark of Arthur Frommer.
Used under license.

Mapping © MAIRDUMONT/Falk Verlag 2008

Cartographic Data © Tele Atlas N.V. 2008 **Tele Atlas**

A03625

ISBN 978-0-4704-5375-9

A CIP catalogue record for this book is available from
the British Library.

The contents of this publication are believed correct
at the time of printing. Nevertheless, the publishers
cannot accept responsibility for errors or omissions,
or for changes in details given in this guide or for
the consequences of any reliance on the information
provided by the same. Assessments of attractions and
so forth are based upon the author's own experience
and, therefore, descriptions given in this guide necessarily
contain an element of subjective opinion which may not
reflect the publishers' opinion or dictate a reader's own
experiences on another occasion.

Colour reproduction by Keene Group, Andover
Printed in China by Leo Paper Group

OPPOSITE: CROWN FOUNTAIN, MILLENNIUM PARK

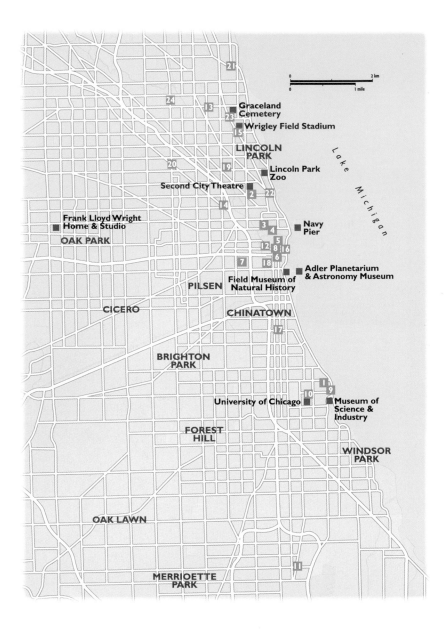

Graceland
Cemetery

Wrigley Field Stadium

LINCOLN
PARK

Lincoln Park
Zoo

Second City Theatre

Lake Michigan

Frank Lloyd Wright
Home & Studio
OAK PARK

Navy
Pier

Adler Planetarium
& Astronomy Museum

Field Museum of
Natural History
PILSEN

CICERO

CHINATOWN

BRIGHTON
PARK

University of Chicago

Museum of
Science &
Industry

FOREST
HILL

WINDSOR
PARK

OAK LAWN

MERRIOETTE
PARK

CONTENTS

Introduction

Chicago, the great city of the American Midwest, is internationally celebrated as a showplace of world-class building and design—most major modern architects have left a calling card in the 'Windy City'. Towering buildings, a lake reaching to the horizon, the rumble of El trains, and weather that can change at the drop of a hat are all facets of Chicago.

One of the city's most enduring symbols is the Municipal Device that can be seen as a way of understanding the complex and schizophrenic nature of Chicago. The device is essentially a Y-shaped figure that can be found all over the city prominently on bridges, electrical boxes, decorative ornamentation on buildings and, most notably, the Chicago Theatre in the Loop. While walking around Chicago, visitors could spend hours playing a version of 'Where's the Municipal Device?' The 'Y' shape is meant to represent the north and south branches of the Chicago River, which winds from Lake Michigan all the way through the north and south sides of Chicago. In a city that's full of cultural and ethnic divisions, it's easy to see how this symbol might also serve as a reminder of the splitting of various groups into distinct neighbourhoods based on a cornucopia of differences.

As a visitor, you can bridge some of these gaps by wandering around different areas on foot, aided by the Chicago Transit Authority (CTA) system of trains and buses. In some ways, the whole experience of taking the elevated train around the city might be best thought of as the unwritten '25th Tour' in this book. Feel free to buy a one-day pass and just jump on a line, go all the way to the end, hop off and see what's around.

Many tours emphasize the Loop (Walks 5, 12, 16, 18) and its diverse attractions and marvels; this book will give you a broad sense of its rich history and transformation over the past century or so. That being said, one must explore the neighbourhoods away from the Loop to get a true sense of the city's pulse. After all, they are where most Chicagoans live, work and play.

Albany Park (Walk 24) is a good place to start exploring, as it has been a popular destination for recent arrivals to the city for over a century, and it remains so in the present day.

Middle Eastern bakeries, thrift stores and Mexican popsicle vendors abound in this area, and, unlike some other Chicago neighbourhoods, it is less ethnically segregated into a monolithic 'Old-World'-style community.

For those looking for something completely different, the Pullman neighbourhood (Walk 11) offers a glimpse into a planned community of the late 19th century. George M. Pullman built the community for his workers and offered them housing, easy access to his nearby train factories for employment, and a sense of community. Things fell apart in 1894,

when a massive strike shut down the factories, leaving Pullman a broken man. It's a rather placid place today, but taking a look around the grounds of this capitalist-styled Utopia provides some interesting insights into the city and the American character. Enjoy your travels around Chicago and don't be afraid to ask questions or move away from the beaten track.

WHERE TO EAT

$	=	Inexpensive
$$	=	Moderate
$$$	=	Expensive

Through the Heart of Hyde Park

Walk through the heart of Hyde Park and discover a village full of free-thinkers, architectural delights and an unforgettable cafeteria.

Hyde Park started life in the 19th century as a place of residence for those who were weary of the hustle and bustle of Chicago, but it has long since been enveloped into the fabric of the city. After stepping off the train at 53rd Street, you get the sense of being in a self-contained urban village. Over the past century the community has served as home to a number of freethinkers and literary types, including Carl Sandburg (1878–1967) and Theodore Dreiser (1871–1945), people associated with the University of Chicago and community activists like Saul Alinsky (1909–72). This tradition continues, and a stop at any of the area's coffee shops confirms that sitting down to discuss both big and small ideas is still a popular pastime here. Two of the main pathways in this racially integrated neighbourhood are 53rd Street and Woodlawn Avenue. This tour takes in the area's oldest house, a cafeteria that doubles as a sociological laboratory and temples built to celebrate commerce and religion.

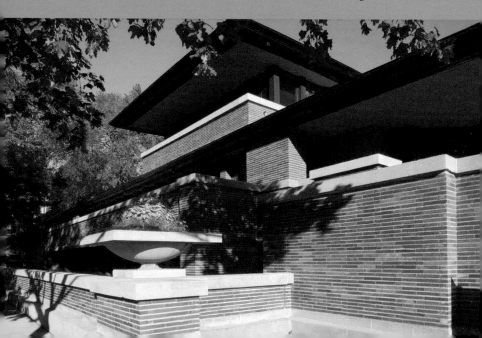

I Exit 53rd Street Metra train station and turn right onto East 53rd Street. Walk across South Lake Park Avenue to the next set of traffic lights. Cross here and pause in front of the Hyde Park Bank Building.

While it may be one of the few bank buildings around in the 1920s that wasn't the victim of a Chicago-style bank robbery, the 11-storey structure has kept a close watch on this corner since 1928. During banking hours, take a moment to walk into the main lobby for a peek. In 2003 the bank set about restoring the interior's lovely marble staircases, polished brass railings and substantial 12ft (3.6m) chandeliers. The building has a formal air, and it's nostalgic to remember a time when going into a bank felt like an occasion of some importance.

2 Walk back across the marked pedestrian crossing (crosswalk) to the north side of East 53rd Street. A few dozen steps to the west is the Valois Cafeteria, a site of sociological enquiry, baked scrod (haddock) and a formidable sign that reads 'See Your Food'.

There are many diners or greasy spoons in Chicago, some of which engage in highly questionable sanitation practices, but there are relatively few cafeterias. Cafeterias are distinguished by the stack of trays near the front of the serving line. At a cafeteria, patrons pick up a tray, order their food, the food goes on the tray and patrons pay at the cash register. The Valois (pronounced 'Val-oyze', not

WHERE TO EAT

[O] VALOIS CAFETERIA,
1518 East 53rd Street;
Tel: 773-667-0647.
Enjoy scrambled eggs and breakfast foods within these mural-painted walls. $

[O] PIZZA CAPRI,
1501 East 53rd Street;
Tel: 773-324-7777.
Pizza and Mediterranean-style salads are the main draws here. $

[O] RIBS 'N BIBS,
5300 South Dorchester Avenue;
Tel: 773-493-0400.
Ribs are the top choice here, but there are other options too. $

in the more regal 'Val-oy' fashion) has been a staple of Hyde Park residents and cafeteria devotees for more than 80 years. Along with corned beef hash and omelettes, the Valois is known for another, more intriguing reason. In the late 1980s, a graduate student at the University of Chicago, Mitch Duneier, came for the food and stayed for the cafeteria's inherent sociological possibilities. He began to observe the middle-aged and elderly men who spent their time at the Valois talking about their lives, their hopes for the future and important issues of the day. Duneier turned his observations into the 1992 book *Slim's Table*, which is well worth picking up.

9

DISTANCE **2 miles (3.2km)**

ALLOW **1.5 hours**

START **Metra commuter rail station on 53rd Street**

FINISH **Metra commuter rail station on 59th Street**

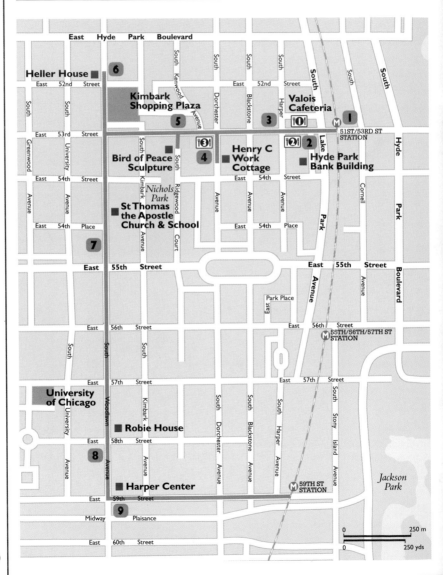

OPPOSITE: THE FRONT VIEW OF HELLER HOUSE, SOUTH WOODLAWN AVENUE

3 After leaving the Valois Cafeteria, walk west on East 53rd Street several blocks to the corner of 53rd Street and South Dorchester Avenue. Use the pedestrian crossing to walk south along Dorchester Avenue. Here you reach Work Cottage at 5317 South Dorchester Avenue.

The modest 19th-century wooden home here is not the Work Cottage. It is actually the building that looks like a more modest addition at the back. As Hyde Park's oldest home, the structure is tiny and quaint. Henry C. Work (1832–84) himself was a well-known composer of Civil War ditties, including *Marching Through Georgia* and the 1876 hit *My Grandfather's Clock*.

4 Walk back up Dorchester Avenue to its intersection with East 53rd Street. Turn left back onto East 53rd Street and walk 70ft (21m) to the west where you will see a short path leading south to Nichols Park, which leads to the Nichols Park Fieldhouse where the *Bird of Peace* sculpture resides.

Dedicated in 1970, the *Bird of Peace* sculpture was crafted by Hyde Park resident Cosmo Campoli (1923–97). Cast in bronze, the sculpture consists of a 5ft (1.5m) bird represented as an egg with a beak and feet. Campoli noted in an interview 'The egg is the most exquisite shape there is. You hold one in your hand and you are holding the whole universe'. Over the years others have felt the same way as Campoli, as community

members have paid to have the egg restored several times after n'er-do-wells have attempted to steal and vandalize this fascinating work of art.

5 Return along the same short path out of Nichols Park to East 53rd Street. Turn left and walk west down East 53rd Street. Walk two blocks past Kimbark Shopping Plaza and turn right onto South Woodlawn Avenue. Walk north a block and a half up Woodlawn Avenue to Heller House at 5132 South Woodlawn Avenue.

As prolific as he was opinionated, architect Frank Lloyd Wright (1867–1959) built a number of buildings in Hyde Park during his life. Completed in 1897, Heller House represents an interesting moment in his career; the building features certain geometric patterns that would become hallmarks of the Prairie School of architecture. The home was constructed with Indiana limestone, which is quite prominent in other residential and institutional buildings throughout Hyde Park.

6 Turn around and walk back down South Woodlawn Avenue to East 53rd Street. Cross the street and walk south on Woodlawn Avenue towards East 55th Street. On the left is St. Thomas the Apostle Church and School.

The design of most Roman Catholic churches in Chicago, and around the world, is meant to emulate the religion's adherence to hierarchy, order and obedience. The architect Barry Byrne (1883–1967) turned those traditions upside down when he designed the forward-thinking structure of St. Thomas in 1924. Inside the church, the worship space is airy, free of columns, and the pews almost bump into the altar. Even if you don't peek inside, admire the ornamental designs on the outside—don't miss the terracotta ornamentation created by Alfonso Iannelli (1888–1965) that graces the western entrance to the church.

7 Walk back to the corner of East 55th Street and Woodlawn Avenue and continue walking south for three blocks. On the way, take a look at some of the grand homes and former (and current) fraternity houses, which mark the eastern boundary of the University of Chicago campus. At the northeast corner of East 58th Street and South Woodlawn Avenue sits Frank Lloyd Wright's architectural paean to the prairie, Robie House.

During the summer months, it's hard to see Robie House among the throngs of tourists who descend upon the world-famous building from motor coaches parked outside the front of the house. It is well worth a look however, as this graceful residence is one of Wright's most compelling works, and remains one of the best-known homes in the world. The building is currently undergoing renovation and reconstruction (due to reopen spring 2010), but visitors can still take an excellent tour of the interior, courtesy of the Frank Lloyd Wright Home and Studio Foundation.

ROBIE HOUSE;

www.gowright.org/robiehouse/robiehouse.htm

8 Walk across East 58th Street to the University of Chicago Graduate School of Business's Harper Center.

Fitting neatly into this small patch of land is a hive of education that's part of the University of Chicago campus. Designed by architect Rafael Vinoly (born 1944), the atrium of this recently completed building pays homage to other Gothic piles on the rest of the campus by its use of curved steel beams that form neat arches. Overall, the atrium has an airy quality that is redolent of other well-thought-out modern light-filled spaces.

9 On leaving the Harper Center, walk south to East 59th Street. Turn left and walk east on East 59th Street four blocks to Metra's 59th Street Station.

ABOVE: *BIRD OF PEACE*, ONE OF HYDE PARK'S BEST-KNOWN SCULPTURES

Cottages, Controversy and Comedy

This tour of the city's oldest residential neighbourhood takes you past tiny cottages, a world-famous comedy club and a 1960s urban renewal project.

Old Town, like many urban 'hoods', has seen a number of second acts. It was an artists' colony in the early part of the 20th century, and before that it was an area of light manufacturing, home to the Dr. Scholl's Shoe Factory. The area became run-down by the 1950s, which attracted poverty-stricken artists and other bohemian types. City leaders like Mayor Richard J. Daley (1902–76) and real estate types like Arthur Rubloff (1902–86) weren't terribly pleased, and by the late 1950s there was growing concern about the area's future. Keeping tabs on 'blight' in post-war Chicago was an obsession of city planners, and Old Town seemed to garner a great deal of attention due to its relative proximity to the Loop. Aggressive redevelopment plans changed the eastern part of Old Town in the 1960s and 1970s, and some breathed a sigh of relief as blight was held in check, at least in this corner of the city. Today, the area's artistic past lives on in the annual Old Town Art Fair held in early June.

1 Exit Chicago Transit Authority's (CTA) Sedgwick stop, pause inside the station entrance to look at the new public art by Carlos 'Dzine' Rolon.

In recent years, the reappearance of public art inside various CTA train stations has brightened up a number of bleak, and at times filthy, transit hubs. After two years of renovation work, Sedgwick station's main entrance opened in late 2007. One of the highlights of the renovation is the very bright and funky *Time is the Enemy* glass panel created by artist Carlos Rolon (born 1970), who is better known by the name Dzine. The CTA allows visitors to take snapshots in public areas, but it's probably not a good idea to poke your camera into the attendant's booth to take a snap.

2 Exit Sedgwick station and turn immediately right to walk south on North Sedgwick Street for about 20 paces. You're now standing in front of Marshall Field Garden Apartments, at the corner of West Blackhawk Street and Sedgwick Street.

Public housing in the United States can be a grim affair, and many people view these urban developments as failed social experiments. Many were built by the lowest bidders and became 'vertical ghettoes' for generations of families. Early public housing started out as a noble experiment, and quickly degenerated into towers of concrete and low maintenance standards. Before the government formally entered this arena in the 1930s,

WHERE TO EAT

⬛1⬛ TWIN ANCHORS,
1655 North Sedgwick Street;
Tel: 312-266-1616.
Frank Sinatra ate here during and after his ring-a-ding-ding years, and the ribs are tasty. $$

⬛2⬛ SALPICON,
1252 North Wells Street;
Tel: 312-988-7811.
This is the place if you are in the mood for grilled tiger shrimp, guacamole and poblano chillies. $$$

⬛3⬛ OLD JERUSALEM,
1411 North Wells Street;
Tel: 312-944-0459.
Enjoy hummus and fine Middle Eastern-style coffee. Outdoor seating during the warmer months. $

there were a number of thoughtful and innovative housing projects created for middle-income residents. The Marshall Field Garden Apartments were just such a project, and when they were completed in 1929, many heralded their arrival as a new model for creating affordable, albeit modest, housing. The tenants took to the buildings with great communal fervour, as they established their own newspaper, performing arts groups and social clubs. These apartments were built to spur redevelopment around this part of Old Town, but it took many decades of private investment to complete the process.

DISTANCE 1.75 miles (2.8km)

ALLOW 2 hours

START CTA train station at Sedgwick Street

FINISH CTA train station at Sedgwick Street

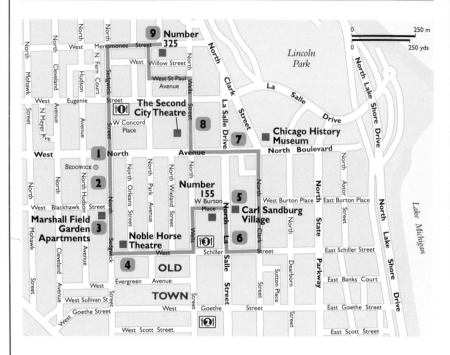

3 Continue walking south on Sedgwick to West Schiller Street, then turn left onto Schiller. Walk east to the northwest corner of North Orleans Street and West Schiller Street. If you missed spotting the horses, you're now right next to Chicago's only remaining riding stables and horse entertainment palace, the Noble Horse Theatre.

Horses fall somewhere behind bikes and unicycles in terms of urban transportation choices for most Americans. When

horse met car a century ago, it was only a matter of time before Ford replaced these hard-working quadrupeds. A few horses graze in the empty lot on Schiller. Some of them work here in the nightly performances inside the Noble Horse Theatre (known for its dramatic use of equines in productions), and others take on the equally gruelling task of carrying visitors up and down North Michigan Avenue on carriage rides. The oldest building dates back to 1871, and the complex was renovated during the turn

of the century. During this renovation, the performance area was enlarged and the main entrance to the theatre reconfigured.

NOBLE HORSE THEATRE;

www.noblehorsechicago.com

4 Turn back onto West Schiller Street and walk east two blocks to North Wells Street, under the CTA's elevated train tracks. At North Wells Street turn left and walk north half-a-block to West Burton Place. Turn right onto Burton Place and you're in the heart of Old Town's historic artists' community.

Today, the urban dwellers of Old Town sport titanium-framed baby strollers and expensive sunglasses, but that wasn't the case 80 years ago. Beginning in the 1920s, Old Town became known as a place for artists to reside and work. The epicentre of the area was this tiny stretch of West Burton Place, then known as

Carl Street. Artists Sol Kogen and Edgar Miller (1899–1993) remodelled Carl Street Studios on 155 West Burton Place during this period. Run your hands over the mosaics and quirky *objets d'art* that decorate the wall that runs along the sidewalk here. Old Town's temporal moment in the vanguard of artistic expression has largely passed, but a look around these buildings is a reminder of the creative spirit that exists in this block.

5 As you leave Burton Place, walk east until you come to North La Salle Street. Cross the street to the east side of North La Salle Street.

This urban development takes it name from the writer who began his career in Chicago. The word 'village' makes most people think of a small swathe of human habitation set amidst verdant surroundings. There's certainly green here during the

DETAIL OF CARVING AROUND THE ENTRANCE OF THE SECOND CITY THEATRE

summer months, but the 1960s and 1970s towers that comprise much of this area are more reminiscent of the city's dwindling supply of notorious large-scale public housing. When Carl Sandburg Village was built it was part of the contentious process of urban renewal, and the whole place is rather uninviting to visitors.

6 Turn right and walk down La Salle Street to West Schiller Street. At Schiller turn left and walk one block to North Clark Street. At Clark Street, turn left and walk two blocks north to the Chicago History Museum, which sits at the northeast corner of West North Avenue and North Clark Street.

From the macabre (the deathbed of Abraham Lincoln (1809–65) to the seemingly mundane (old manholes), the Chicago History Museum contains pieces of ephemera collected from every era of the city's past. The dioramas depicting infamous events such as the Chicago Fire of 1871 are worth a look, and rotating exhibits have included an exploration of Chicago's parochial school system and a visual tribute to the rock band Chicago.

CHICAGO HISTORY MUSEUM;
www.chicagohistory.org

7 Walk two blocks west on West North Avenue to North Wells Street. Cross to the west side and walk to the The Second City Theatre.

If you're in front of an architectural frieze that looks like it was slapped onto another building, you're in the right place. This stretch of Wells Street was once a haven for creative types, occasional hippies and a bit of counterculture. In the 1950s, the improvisational comedy cabal known as 'Second City' came north from the South Side to set up shop on Wells Street. Their number included Alan Arkin, Joan Rivers and the inimitable Del Close, who would create the improvisational structure known as the 'Harold'. Their shows always seem to have creative titles: *Freud Slipped Here, Orwell That Ends Well.*

THE SECOND CITY THEATRE;
www.secondcity.com/

8 Continue north on North Wells Street for one and a half blocks. Turn left onto West St Paul Avenue and continue to North Park Avenue. At North Park Avenue turn right, and walk two blocks north to West Menomonee Street. Turn right on West Menomonee and stop in front of the cottages at 325 West Menomonee Street.

These modest cottages offer visitors a sense of what this section of Old Town looked like prior to the Great Chicago Fire of 1871. In fact, the cottage at 348 West Menomonee is a fire relief cottage, a building that was placed on a wagon and moved to an empty lot as a form of temporary housing for those displaced by the conflagration.

9 Walk west on West Menomonee to North Sedgwick Avenue. Turn left and go south across West North Avenue to return to CTA's Sedgwick station.

A TERRACE OF BRICK AND WOODEN RESIDENCES IN OLD TOWN'S TRIANGLE NEIGHBOURHOOD

The Gold Coast: Luxury by Lake Michigan

Stretch your legs and take this stroll through the Gold Coast, where you will find some of the city's most historic residences.

This tour includes the grand residence of Chicago's Roman Catholic Archbishop, a stroll near Lake Michigan and a look at the austere building that was once the swinging Playboy Mansion. The 19th-century retail magnate Potter Palmer (1826–1902) and his wife Bertha (1849–1918) gave the area the initial gold standard when they built their massive mansion on North Lake Shore Drive in 1882. The members of Chicago's social register took a hint, and mansions popped up around the area like mushrooms after heavy rain. The area was fashionable through the 20th century, though many older homes were demolished to accommodate modern residences. While some of the new buildings were inventive and thoughtful, most of them were pedestrian exercises in modernism. Nevertheless, the Gold Coast retains its powerful social cachet, and on a pleasant day can be a respite from the tourist-drenched Magnificent Mile.

I From the CTA's Clark and Division Station, walk to the north side of West Division Street. Proceed east for two blocks to the corner of North State Parkway and West Division Street. Cross to the east side of North State Parkway and walk north for about 20 paces to 1209 North State Parkway.

After walking along the row of bars in West Division Street, it's refreshing to reach a cultural and architectural oddity in the form of the Frank Fisher Studio Houses. Built in 1937, the houses stand out in the Gold Coast because they are in the Art Moderne idiom and were built during the Great Depression—when there wasn't a whole lot of building going on anywhere. It's worth taking a peek into the landscaped courtyard before moving on. Here visitors will see elaborate gardens (at their best in spring and summer) and a peaceful nook tucked away amid the fracas that exists just a Martini glass toss across Division Street.

2 Walk south back to the intersection of West Division Street and North State Parkway. Turn left and go east on East Division Street. At the northwest corner of East Division Street and North Lake Shore Drive—the street, not the multilane highway beyond the local road —is 1200 North Lake Shore Drive.

This notable residential structure represents a transitional time in the Gold Coast's historical development, and was the first and last word in such dwellings when it was finished in 1913.

WHERE TO EAT

🍽 **THIRD COAST CAFÉ,**
1260 North Dearborn Street;
Tel: 312-649-0730.
This low-key café is good for all-day breakfast or brunch, and their coffee is nice and strong. $$

🍽 **ZEBRA LOUNGE,**
1220 North State Parkway;
Tel: 312-642-5140.
Tucked into an unassuming apartment building, the Zebra is well known for its piano bar and dedicated patrons. Show up early to get a seat for the evening. $$

🍽 **TIPAROS THAI CUISINE,**
1540 North Clark Street;
Tel: 312-712-9900.
Good massaman curry, and try their bubble tea. $

Up to that point, most of the residential buildings were large and stately 19th-century homes of the wealthy. Whereas 1200 North Lake Shore offered luxury apartments in the sky, complete with a classy entrance on East Division Street.

3 Keep walking north on the west side of North Lake Shore Drive two blocks to the solidly built Carl C. Heisen House at 1250 North Lake Shore Drive.

This is how the rich really lived, and some still like it just fine. Before the vertical towers came to the Gold Coast

23

DISTANCE **2 miles (3.2km)**

ALLOW **2 hours**

START **CTA train station at Clark and Division**

FINISH **CTA bus stop at corner of West North Avenue and North Clark**

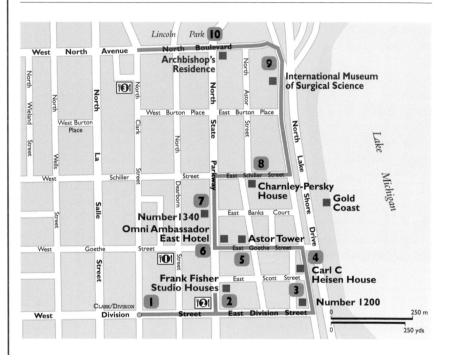

in the 1910s and 1920s, it was a mark of Chicago's upper crust to build a signature house along Lake Shore Drive. It was certainly more pleasant before the state highway arrived in 1937. The Heisen House was built in 1890 in the Richardsonian Romanesque style—distinquished by its use of ponderous massing of forms such as medieval-style arches and cylindrical towers—and a century later it was joined to its neighbour at 1254 North Lake Shore Drive through a series of renovations intended to increase its desirability and in a nod to the demands of modern urban dwellers.

4 Go north on North Lake Shore Drive to East Goethe Street. Turn left on East Goethe Street and walk west to North Astor Place. At the northwest corner of North Astor Place and East Goethe is the modernist Astor Tower.

The construction of this well-executed minor modernist masterpiece by Bertrand Goldberg (1913-97) caused a tempest in

OPPOSITE: THE GOLD COAST, LOOKING NORTH TO LINCOLN PARK

the teapots of Gold Coast residents back in 1963. They were dismayed that the city allowed developers to build the 25-floor hotel in an area that consisted primarily of low-rise homes. The building went up despite complaints, and it is now an apartment building. Peering up the side of the building, visitors should pay attention to the permanent metal fixtures that screen the glass windows.

5 **Continue to walk west on the north side of East Goethe Street. After 200ft (60m), you'll be in front of the Omni Ambassador East Hotel.**

Over the past decades, the Ambassador East has seen lots of glamorous guests pass through its main entrance. Many of them made a beeline for the hotel's fabled Pump Room. The Pump Room takes its name from a gathering place in Bath, England, which was known to play host to such noble guests as Queen Anne and others escaping from London for a holiday respite. The hotel itself has been captured in a few notable films, including *North by Northwest,* and some less notable ones, such as *Straight Talk* with Dolly Parton and James Woods.

6 **Continue west to the corner of East Goethe Street and North State Parkway. Cross to the west side of North State Parkway. Walk north on State Parkway to the sober-looking house at 1340 North State Parkway.**

The most famous resident of this building was Hugh Hefner (born 1926), jazz lover

and publisher of *Playboy* magazine. As a Chicago native, Hefner loved to draw and worked as a copywriter for *Esquire* before starting *Playboy* in 1953. He laid out the first issue of the magazine in his Hyde Park apartment, and after a few years of healthy sales was a very wealthy individual. He purchased 1340 North State Parkway in 1959, and it quickly became known as 'the Playboy Mansion'. Hefner was reputed to wander around his 48-room home wearing Bunnygirl-trademark pyjamas as he worked on each issue. After a time, jazz sessions and late-night parties were staple activities. Hef decamped for Southern California permanently in the 1970s, and donated the building to the Art Institute of Chicago. It was turned into private residences, so best not to knock on the door and expect to find any bunnies or other trappings of the Playboy lifestyle.

7 **Walk north on North State Parkway to East Schiller Street. Turn right onto Schiller Street and walk east to North Astor Place. On the southeast corner of North Astor Place and Schiller Street sits the Charnley–Persky House.**

The Charnley–Persky House is the meeting of two magnificent architectural minds, Louis Sullivan (1856–1924) and Frank Lloyd Wright. Wright was primarily responsible for the design, as he was in the employ of the firm of Adler and Sullivan at the time the house was built in 1892. Sullivan was the supervising architect on the project, and Wright lent his talents in thinking about the building's interior

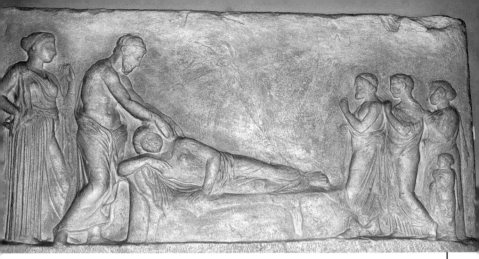

design. Currently it serves as the home of the Society of Architectural Historians, and visitors can ring the doorbell and take a peek inside. Free tours of the home are offered on Wednesday at noon.
CHARNLEY–PERSKY HOUSE;
www.charnleyhouse.org/

8 Walk east on East Schiller Street to North Lake Shore Drive. At North Lake Shore Drive, walk north past East Burton Place to the International College of Surgeons museum.

Run by the International College of Surgeons, who occupy the neoclassical pile of bricks on North Lake Shore Drive, the International Museum of Surgical Science is a find, largely overlooked by tourists. In the past, it has featured exhibits on the history of orthopaedics, polio and that oh-so-popular subject, plastic surgery.
INTERNATIONAL MUSEUM OF SURGICAL SCIENCE;
www.imss.org/

9 Continue north on North Lake Shore Drive for about two minutes. Cars can't turn west here, but people on foot can cross the grass to a cul-de-sac to West North Boulevard. Walk west on North Avenue to the corner of North State Parkway and West North Boulevard. On the southeast corner of the intersection is the residence of the Roman Catholic Archbishop of Chicago.

This humble domicile is where the Archbishop of Chicago hangs his mitre. Look up at the busy roofline, which contains a staggering number of chimneys. Immediately behind the residence is one of Chicago's remaining wooden block-paved alleys, a reminder of the city's previous mode of road construction; there are only a couple left in the entire city.

10 Walk two blocks west on West North Avenue to return to the northwest corner of North Clark Street and North Avenue to catch the number 22 Clark or 36 Broadway bus.

River North: Light Industry to Not-So-Light Shopping

You'll get a sense of the rich history of the River North community by lingering at some of the fascinating points of interest you pass on this tour.

The area started life as Chicago's first industrial hub, when the Chicago River was a transportation corridor for boats carrying freight and industrial supplies. As the river became less important for transporting goods, the area went into a slow and steady decline, with rail and elaborate roadways overtaking the river as conduits for moving goods and people. Artists and other creative folk rediscovered the area in the 1970s and began converting the old warehouses and factories that dotted the area into galleries and loft spaces. The 1980s and 1990s saw the arrival of a slew of somewhat anonymous chain restaurants, such as the Hard Rock Café, in the heart of the neighbourhood, and an increasing phalanx of suburban day-trippers. River North has a great deal to offer in terms of history and compelling architecture.

1 Exit the bus at the intersection of West Hubbard Street and North Dearborn Street, and walk west along the north side of West Hubbard Street to the main entrance of the (former) Cook County Criminal Court Building at 54 West Hubbard Street.

This staid-looking building's primary purpose is now business rather than justice. From 1893 to 1929, it was the home of the Cook County Criminal Courts and saw plenty of action, legally speaking. Famed egghead killers Nathan Leopold (1904–71) and Richard A. Loeb (1905–36) went on trial here in 1924 for the murder of Bobby Franks (1909–24) in a case that was billed as the 'Trial of the Century'. Leopold and Loeb had kidnapped young Franks and murdered him in cold blood, and they were defended by legendary jurist Clarence Darrow (1857–1938). The trial of members of the 1919 Chicago White Sox occurred here, it was known as the 'Black Sox Scandal'. This involved a number of members of the White Sox baseball team who had conspired to throw the 1919 World Series to the Cincinnati Reds.

2 Turn back to walk east on West Hubbard Street for one block to North State Street. On State Street, cross to the east side and walk north for three blocks to the northeast corner of North State Street and East Ohio Street.

Long before anyone was talking about formally supporting artists in the city, Judge Lambert Tree (1832–1910) and his wife Anne were working on creating an artists' colony in this corner of the city in the early 1890s. In 1894 when the Tree Studios were up and running, artists lived and worked in the building at subsidized rates, and over the years a number of prominent muralists, sculptors and painters including John Warner Norton (1876–1934) and Pauline Palmer (1867–1938) called the building home. Artists are no longer here, and the retail mix currently includes a wine bar.

3 Walk one block on East Ohio Street to the northwest corner of North Wabash Street and Ohio Street. Here is the mystical, magical Medinah Temple.

The Shriners are an organization rooted in curious initiation ceremonies, known for their unusual headwear and their worldwide burn hospitals. This building is a testimony to their immense popularity and financial prowess in the early 20th century, and presents a whirlwind tour of

DISTANCE **2.25 miles (3.6km)**

ALLOW **2 hours**

START **CTA bus stop at North Dearborn Street and West Hubbard**

FINISH **CTA bus stop at North Clark Street and West Oak Street**

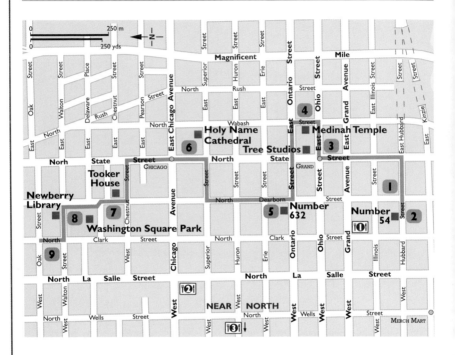

Middle Eastern-influenced architectural ornamentation—its arches and intricate details are magnificent. Notice the stylized plants and geometric forms known as 'arabesques'. Today it houses Bloomingdale's, as the Shriners have decamped to the suburbs of Chicago.

4 Walk north on North Wabash Street for one block, then turn left onto East Ontario Street. Walk back past the north side of the Tree Studios, cross North State Street and continue

west on Ontario Street to the northwest corner of North Dearborn Street and Ontario Street. At this corner you will find the former Chicago Historical Society building, 632 North Dearborn Street.

If you wanted a building to hold a city's historical treasures (such as Abraham Lincoln's deathbed, now in the Chicago History Museum), you probably couldn't do better than this weighty Romanesque Revival building. Designed by architect

Henry Ives Cobb (1859–1931), the building was the home of the Chicago Historical Society until 1931. After the Society moved to Lincoln Park, the building was used as the home of the Institute of Design and recording studios. Today, the building houses a dance club.

5 Walk north on North Dearborn Street to the corner of Dearborn Street and West Superior Street. Cross to the north side of Superior Street and turn right to walk one block east to the northeast corner of North State Street and East Superior Street.

Holy Name Cathedral has a prominent place in the hearts of many Catholic Chicagoans, as it is the seat of the Roman Catholic Archdiocese of Chicago. The current edifice on the site was dedicated in 1875, and it features a 210ft (64m) spire. Take a look at the impressive bronze front doors on the front of the cathedral.

6 Continue north on North State Street for two blocks. At West Chestnut Street, turn left and go one block west to North Dearborn Street. Turn north on North Dearborn Street and continue to the Robert N. Tooker House at 863 North Dearborn Street.

The Tooker House has a rosy granite façade, which adds to the appeal of this clutch of town homes across the street

from Washington Square. The real treat here is Tooker Place (no sign), which is on the alley next to the house. Back in the 1920s and 1930s visitors walked down this alley to the main entrance to the Dill Pickle Club, where noted anarchists, rabble-rousers and characters like Carl Sandburg came to discuss social issues of the day. The motto on the club's door reads 'Step High, Stoop Low, Leave Your Dignity Outside'.

7 Cross west over North Dearborn Street to Washington Square Park.

If you are pining for debate and dialogue after the Dill Pickle Club, Washington Square Park might be just the tonic. The park started life as a genteel public square with a central fountain and well-placed benches. In the early decades of the 20th century, it became known as 'Bughouse Square', as various residents of the nearby rooming houses came to debate, harangue and argue amid these bucolic surroundings.

8 Exit Washington Square Park and cross to the corner of North Dearborn Street and West Walton Street. On the northwest corner sits the Newberry Library.

Established as part of a bequest from Walter Loomis Newberry, the Newberry Library has over 21 miles (34km) of books, maps and manuscripts squirrelled away in its main building and a subsequent addition created by Harry Weese (1915–98) and associates in 1981. Some

WHERE TO EAT

🍽 **LA MADIA,**
59 West Grand Avenue;
Tel: 312-329-0400.
A haute-pizza restaurant where it's thin crust all the way and you can watch the chefs in action. $$

🍽 **CAFÉ IBERICO,**
739 North La Salle Street;
Tel: 312-573-1510.
The sangria flows freely at this popular tapas bar, but it can be difficult to get a table at the weekend. $$$

🍽 **CLUB LAGO,**
331 West Superior Street;
Tel: 312-337-9444.
A treat if you are in the mood for calamari and chicken cacciatore. $$

of the items in the collection include the archives of the Illinois Central Railroad Company and the Edward E. Ayer Collection of American Indian History. The library is open to the public and, along with the bookstore, has free exhibits covering the history of cartography, exploration and related matters.

NEWBERRY LIBRARY;
www.newberry.org/

9 After leaving the Newberry, turn right and walk west to North Clark Street. At North Clark Street, turn right and go north to the CTA bus stop just south of West Oak Street.

THE WRIGLEY BUILDING FORMS A STUNNING BACKDROP FOR MICHIGAN AVENUE BRIDGE

Along the Chicago River, River Loop

A walk along the Chicago River in the Loop tells the background story of the city's hopes and dreams in brick, steel and glass.

From Michigan Avenue Bridge to the art deco-styled Civic Opera House, this walk takes you along the buildings and structures that define this corner of the Loop. Much of the city's history can be read—in one fashion or another—through the Michigan Avenue Bridge. The bridge hitched the aspirations of the area north of the river to those of the Loop, and a few years after its construction the vacant lots began filling up with new commercial and retail buildings. Transport across the river grew exponentially with the bridge's completion, and other modern bridges began to span the river. Soon, every major player in the real estate business wanted a signature building along the river, and by the 1980s there were few open spaces left that fronted directly onto the water. Buildings such as Marina City Towers and 333 Wacker Drive respond to the river in different ways through the use of materials that include rough concrete and shiny slippery façades of reflective glass, but taken together they offer a fine portrait of the area's development and architectural transformation.

After getting off the bus on North Michigan Avenue, walk north across the street, but not across the bridge, to the northeast corner of North Michigan Avenue and East Wacker Drive.

The basic function of a bridge is to help people and vehicles move from one place to another smoothly. Some bridges accomplish this with great architectural aplomb, while others are unadorned and downright functional. Built in 1926, the Michigan Avenue Bridge manages to succeed on both counts. The original plan for spanning the Chicago River took root in the Chicago Plan of 1909, which correctly surmised that such a feat of engineering would spur development on the north side of the river bank. The bridge remains an iconic structure, consistently appearing in television programmes, and it has popped up on celluloid a number of times, including the 1987 film *The Untouchables*. Take a moment to look at the pylons on the south side of the bridge; they offer a sculptural tour through a few key events in Chicago history, including the siege of Fort Dearborn and the exploration of the region in the 17th century by Father Marquette.

2 Walk south across East Wacker Drive and cross over North Michigan Avenue to the southwest corner of Upper Wacker Drive and Michigan Avenue.

When skyscrapers began to pop up around this bend in the Chicago River

WHERE TO EAT

🍴 SALVADOR'S BARRO,
73 East Lake Street;
Tel: 312-346-8457.
This Mexican cantina comes with cacti-decor and salt-rimmed margaritas. $$

🍴 PETTERINO'S,
150 North Dearborn Street;
Tel: 312-422-0150.
This clubby surf-and-turf place draws in the theatre crowd. It's pricey but a fine choice for an upmarket night out. $$$

🍴 MONK'S PUB,
205 West Lake Street;
Tel: 312-357-6665.
The burgers are worth a stop. This Loop tavern caters to the after-work crowd and some loyal regulars. $

in the 1920s, some city planners and architects wondered how these new buildings would respond to both the Chicago River and the surrounding structures. The London Guarantee & Accident Building at 360 North Michigan Avenue features a graceful entrance and a series of columns that make the building look like a birthday cake. Outside the main entrance, you can learn about the long-gone Fort Dearborn that once stood on this site.

3 Cross to the north side of East Wacker Drive. Continue walking

DISTANCE 1.8 miles (2.9km)

ALLOW 1.5 hours

START CTA bus stop at North Michigan Avenue and East Upper Wacker Drive

FINISH CTA train station at West Washington Street and North Wells Street

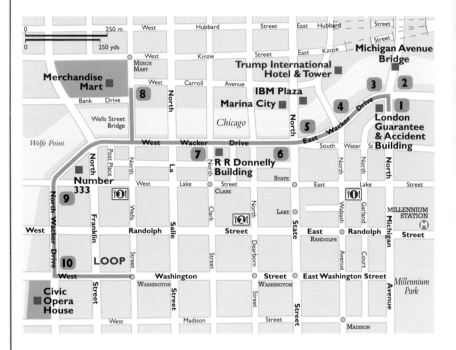

west on Wacker Drive (at street level, not down by the pedestrian walkway) for about 100ft (30m). Look north across the Chicago River to the Trump International Hotel and Tower.

Donald Trump (born 1946) never met an oversized project he didn't like, and the Trump International Hotel was his first excursion into the rough-and-tumble world of Chicago real estate. The 96-floor tower replaced the former squat home of the *Chicago Sun-Times* newspaper.

The building features three prominent setbacks and responds appropriately to the angled piece of land it occupies.

4 Continue walking west on Wacker Drive for a block to the intersection of North State Street and Wacker Drive. Look across the Chicago River to Marina City and the IBM Plaza.

Iconic even before they were finished, the Marina City Towers bear an uncanny resemblance to a pair of corncobs. When

6 Cross to the south side of Wacker Drive. Continue walking west for two blocks to the southeast corner of Wacker Drive and North Clark Street. Here stands the R. R. Donnelly Building.

Peering up to the top of the building 49 floors high, it's hard to think that an architect would attempt to bring together classical Rome with the shiny glass exteriors of the modern skyscraper. In 1992 Ricardo Bofill (born 1939), the noted Spanish architect, created this building from a mix of architectural styles, but in a postmodern world anything is possible. You will note that the building appears to resemble a Classical courthouse plopped on top of an oversized structure dedicated to the finest commercial pursuits around.

the towers were finished in 1964, they were the tallest residential buildings in the world. The first 19 floors are used for parking, and floors 21 to 60 contain apartments. The 20th floor of each structure contains a laundry room with panoramic views of the surrounding area. Today, the complex also contains a House of Blues music venue, which is located in the odd saddle-shaped building behind the towers, alongwith a pricey bowling alley and several high-end restaurants.

7 Walk west on West Wacker Drive for two blocks to the intersection of Wacker Drive and North Wells Street. At North Wells Street, walk north and cross the Wells Street bridge to reach the Merchandise Mart.

5 Cross the street to the east to 330 North Wabash.

For many years this was known as IBM Plaza. The boxy building was the last commission of Mies van der Rohe (1886–1969) in the United States, and was completed after his death in 1971. Recently, plans were announced to turn the building into another hotel, to join the plethora along the Chicago River.

In a city that is known for superlatives, the Merchandise Mart most certainly contributes its share of outsized statistics. After its completion in 1930, the building was the largest in the world, and even today it maintains over 4 million sq ft (371,600sq m) of rentable space. Originally built as a wholesale store for the Marshall Field Company, the building was owned by the Kennedy family until 1998. Walk inside the main entrance to the building along the river to catch a glimpse of the murals by Jules Guérin (1886–1946), which depict the history of trade through the ages.

8 Walk south back across the Wells Street bridge to the intersection of North Wells Street and West Wacker Drive. Turn right and walk west on Wacker Drive for one block until coming to 333 Wacker Drive.

This office building marks the northwest corner of the Loop, and its curved wall of green glass faces directly onto the Chicago River. On a sunny day, it is a sight to see the nearby buildings reflected in its façade, and the building has been a local favourite since its completion in 1983. Directly across from the building sits a stub of land known as Wolfe Point, which marks the beginning of the north branch of the Chicago River.

9 Continue walking south on North Wacker Drive to the southwest corner of West Washington Street and Wacker Drive. This block is occupied by the Civic Opera House.

Utilities tycoon Samuel Insull (1859-1938) constructed this magisterial art deco building in 1929. Insull had no small plans when he built the structure, as he hoped that it would be a performance space for his wife, Gladys, who was not particularly well regarded for her vocal stylings. The building has served as the home of the Lyric Opera of Chicago since 1954, and is the second largest opera auditorium in North America.

10 Walk two blocks east on Washington Street to the CTA station at the intersection of Washington Street and North Wells Street.

ILLUMINATED BUILDINGS LINING THE CHICAGO RIVER AT NIGHT, WITH THE MERCHANDISE MART ON THE LEFT

That Great Street: State Street's Architecture

A walk down State Street takes you through the city's retail past and present, with glimpses into the bright lights of the entertainment district.

Frank Sinatra (1915–98) sang about State Street being 'great street', but it came from humble beginnings, as it was originally the main route south through the state of Illinois. By the late 19th century major retailers had flagship stores here and until the mid-1940s, State Street was the place to shop and play in the Loop. People flocked to see the large window displays at Christmas and visit the theatres scattered up and down the street. By the 1950s, developments along North Michigan Avenue north of the Chicago River threatened the retail supremacy of State Street. The 'Magnificent Mile' ruled with an iron fist of shiny new buildings and upmarket shops, and State Street couldn't compete. The process of suburbanization and reliance on the automobile, and the declining fortunes of the retail environment in this area, dealt a mean punch to State Street and by the 1970s it was down for the count. Creating a new pedestrian mall didn't help; the mall concept was swept away in 1996 and new planters and historic markers were added to create a bit of urban Renaissance along State Street.

1 Step off the bus at the CTA stop near the southeast corner of South State Street and East Van Buren Street. On this corner sits the Second Leiter Building.

Levi Leiter (1834–1904) was a pioneering Chicago retailer who was also the business partner of Marshall Field, a giant in the annals of department store fame. In 1891 he commissioned William LeBaron Jenney (1832–1907) to create this building. Later it became the flagship department store of Sears, Roebuck & Company. Today, the building is a Chicago landmark and mainly occupied by a college. The First Leiter Building met an untimely end via a wrecking ball in 1972. This was unfortunate, as the building represented one of the first true 'skyscrapers' in every sense of the word. At five (later seven) storeys, it had an iron skeletal frame, vertical transportation in the form of elevators, and fireproofing materials.

2 Walk south on the east side of State Street along the Second Leiter Bulding. At the corner of East Congress Parkway and South State Street, cross to the west side of the street. It's hard to miss the Harold Washington Library as it takes up almost an entire city block.

Harold Washington (1922–87) was the city's first African-American mayor. Elected in 1983, Mayor Washington took charge of a city that was faced with many problems, including racial strife, decaying infrastructure and a declining population. During his two terms in office, Washington was able to bring a measure

of reform and stability to a city that had been racked by political patronage and corruption for decades. Washington died of a heart attack, and the city mourned his passing. Several years later, the city approved funding for a new central library, and given Washington's love of reading, it was fitting that the new building should be named after him. Opened in 1991, this huge neoclassical building contains nods to architecture of Chicago's past with the sheer massiveness of its architectural ornamentation and imposing presence.

3 Walk north on State Street for one block to the intersection with East Jackson Boulevard. Walk east across State Street to the southeast corner of State Street and Jackson Boulevard to the front of the DePaul Center.

For most of the 20th century this grand building was the former Rothschild & Company department store, and then

DISTANCE 1 mile (1.6km)

ALLOW 1.5 hours

START CTA bus stop near South State Street and East Van Buren Street

FINISH CTA train station at Lake Street and State Street

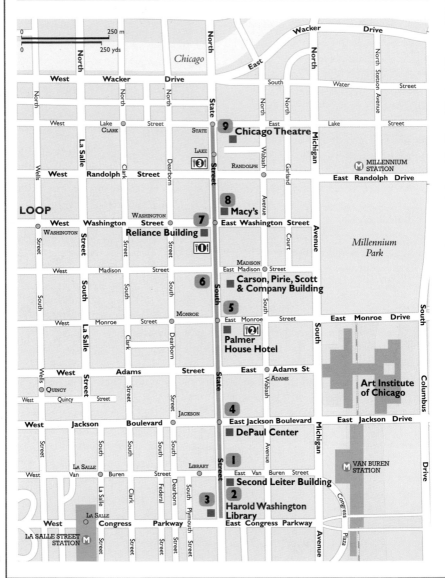

the Goldblatt department store later in the century. In the late 1980s the large department store at this location was on its last legs, and the building was finally purchased by the city. DePaul University, a local Roman Catholic university, was looking to expand in the Loop, and purchased the building and spent many millions renovating the structure. The plaza out front is a good place to linger a while and people-watch.

4 Walk north on the east side of State Street for two blocks to the southeast corner with East Monroe Street. Here you'll see the Palmer House Hotel at 17 East Munroe Street.

The first Palmer House Hotel on this site didn't have an auspicious beginning. Three weeks after its completion in 1871, the Great Chicago Fire swept through the area, leaving just a pile of embers. Potter Palmer hired architect John M. Van Osdel (1811–91) to build a new luxury hotel to add to the growing number already in the Loop. The current hotel

was built on the same site as the first two hotels, completed in 1927. Walking into the lobby, take in the sumptuous and detailed paintings that cover every inch of the ceiling. Currently the hotel is undergoing a renovation, which will no doubt restore some of its former glory and polish.

5 Continue north on State Street to the southeast corner of State Street and East Madison Street.

Standing at what was referred to as the 'busiest corner in the world' in the 19th century, the Carson, Pirie, Scott & Company Building stands as the living embodiment of the forward-thinking architectural principles of Louis Sullivan (1856–1924). Throughout his productive career, Sullivan adhered to his credo of 'form ever follows function', but in the Scott building he did not follow this mantra. Along the main entrance reach out and touch some of his geometric designs. The cast-iron work is superb, and every glance will reveal something new.

6 Cross over to the west side of State Street and walk north one block to the southwest corner of West Washington Street and State Street.

The Reliance Building is the great-grandfather of today's glass-and-steel towers. Certainly not all of this fabulous building's progeny have been executed with such finesse, but the light and airy terracotta exterior of the 15 storeys wowed Chicagoans in the Gay 1890s.

7 Walk north across West Washington Street. Cross east across State Street to the northeast corner of West Washington Street and State Street.

The dry goods business in Chicago was where many future retail giants started, and Marshall Field (1834–1906) was among their number when he arrived from Massachusetts in the 1850s. After building a number of structures for his growing business, Field eventually consolidated his retail operations with this flagship building on State Street. The store eventually expanded to cover this entire city block. The highlights here include the Great Clocks along the outside of the building and the Louis Tiffany & Company mosaic dome located in the store's southwest corner. In 2006 the Marshall Field name disappeared from Chicago as Macy's purchased the chain and renamed the remaining stores.

8 Continue north on State Street, passing East Randolph Street, to the Chicago Theatre.

WHERE TO EAT

🍽 **ATWOOD CAFÉ,**
1 West Washington Street;
Tel: 312-368-1900.
Located in the lobby of the Reliance Building, the Atwood Café serves nouvelle American cuisine and tea service on weekday afternoons. $$$

🍽 **MILLER'S PUB & RESTAURANT,**
134 South Wabash Avenue;
Tel: 312-263-4988.
Ribs and burgers are excellent options and the bar scene is friendly. $$

🍽 **ARGO TEA,**
16 West Randolph Street;
Tel: 312-553-1550.
This Chicago-based tea retailer serves tea (naturally), baked goods and a small selection of sandwiches. $

The wildly lavish interior of this movie palace allowed visitors to slip away from their everyday lives into comedy, drama and romance, which seemed for a moment to be larger than life. Finished in 1921, the building was designed by theatre architects par excellence, Rapp & Rapp. There are tours available of the building's interior.

CHICAGO THEATRE;
www.thechicagotheatre.com/

9 Walk north one block to the CTA's train station at the intersection of Lake and State Street.

Hizzoner's Greatest Achievement

Stroll through the mid-20th-century landscape of the University of Illinois to the largely late-19th-century urban milieu that constitutes Little Italy.

This tour features tons of poured concrete, a bustling lemonade stand and enough *prosciutto* to feed many mouths. Starting off with a visit to Jane Addams' Hull House, it winds its way into the heart of the University of Illinois at Chicago (UIC) campus. Mayor Richard J. Daley (1902–76), known as 'Hizzoner', was set on utilizing this site to create a massive public urban university for the citizens of Chicago. Parts of Little Italy stood in his way but, despite a range of citizen protests, construction of the campus began in 1963. Walking out of the campus, you are now in the heart of Little Italy, and the architecture consists largely of three-storey residential buildings, churches, restaurants and other retail spots. Taylor Street is the main thoroughfare, and this street in the summertime can be a delight. The area was never exclusively Italian, and even today you will witness aspects of Latino and African-American culture.

After hopping off the CTA bus on South Halsted Street, you'll be right in front of the Hull-House Museum. It's hard to miss the building as it sits rather conspicuously in front of the concrete-clad entrance to the University of Illinois at Chicago campus.

Jane Addams (1860–1935) was one of the most prominent social reformers of the 19th and 20th centuries, and after growing up in rural Illinois she came to the wicked city of Chicago to begin her professional life as an individual bent on assisting the city's immigrant population. She came to work in the city's Near West Side right here on Halsted Street, and until her death in 1935 she was a tireless crusader for the rights of the poor. During that time she began to create the Hull House organization, which provided a wide range of services to nearby residents. All that remains today of the original Hull House complex is right here, and the museum is well worth a visit.

HULL-HOUSE MUSEUM;

www.uic.edu/jaddams/hull

2 Walk west through the Chicago Circle Center building and continue west for about 100ft (30m) to the landscaped plaza that marks the centre of this portion of the campus.

After walking through the main student union building, one gets a sense of what the architecture at the University of Illinois at Chicago campus is all about, namely no-holds barred modernism. Here in the central plaza of the East Campus, you can see the main lecture halls on campus, along with the Richard J. Daley Library, which lies directly to the west. This plaza once contained a sunken amphitheatre, which was dreadfully windy in the winter and brutally hot in the summer. It is not missed on campus, and students seem to enjoy the current configuration a great deal.

3 Continue walking west to the Richard J. Daley Library. Depending on the hour, you can walk through the library to South Morgan Street, or you may need to walk north around the library and proceed west to South

DISTANCE **2.2 miles (3km)**

ALLOW **2.5 hours**

START **CTA bus stop on South Halsted Street**

FINISH **CTA train station at Paulina and West Polk Street**

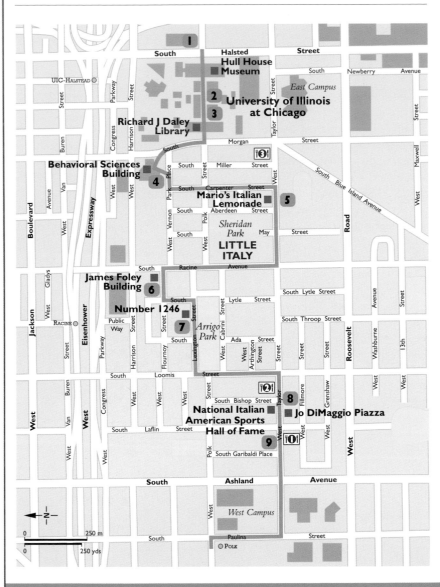

OPPOSITE: THE ITALIAN NEIGHBOURHOOD KNOWN AS LITTLE ITALY

WHERE TO EAT

🍴 POMPEI,
1531 West Taylor Street;
Tel: 312-421-5179.
After a century in Little Italy, Pompei remains a reliable choice for pizza, salads and pasta dishes. $

🍴 CONTE DE SAVOIA,
1438 West Taylor Street;
Tel: 312-666-3471.
In this tightly packed Italian deli, the *prosciutto* sandwich is always a fine choice for a lunch in the nearby Joe DiMaggio Piazza. $

🍴 TUSCANY RESTAURANT,
1014 West Taylor Street;
Tel: 312-829-1990.
Torn jeans or other such attire won't fly at this genteel Italian favourite that offers excellent roasted chicken and fine sorbets imported from Milan. $$$

Morgan Street. Upon reaching Morgan Street, walk north to West Vernon Park Place. At West Vernon Park Place, walk west a few steps to the Behavioral Sciences Building.

Depending on your sense of humour, this building is either a cruel joke perpetuated on unsuspecting undergraduates or just an effective form of human mousetrap. The building has twists and turns galore and, if it's open, take the challenge to see if you can navigate your way out.

4 After leaving the Behavioral Sciences Building, turn right and continue walking west on Vernon Park Place. On the south side of the street sits a cul-de-sac that leads to South Carpenter Street. Cross south over Vernon Park Place and walk two blocks south on Carpenter Street to West Taylor Street. Turn right onto Taylor Street and continue walking west for a few paces until you spy a red, white and green hut that says 'Mario's Italian Lemonade'.

They don't call it Little Italy for nothing, and despite the fact that immigration from Italy to Chicago has slowed to a trickle in the 21st century there are a few reminders of the area's ethnic heritage around Taylor Street. Mario's is one such vestige of this past, and their Italian lemonade is a perfect treat on a spring or summer afternoon. Cops, locals, tourists, schoolchildren and others all make regular stops here, and right across the street is Al's Italian Beef, another area favourite. For those who aren't fond of Italian ice, Mario's also offers nuts, candy and *lupini* beans.

5 Walk west on West Taylor Street for two blocks. At South Racine Avenue, turn right and walk two blocks north to Flournoy Street. Cross over Racine Avenue to the northwest corner of Flournoy Street and Racine Avenue.

The James Foley Building at this corner is fairly typical for the late 1880s, and it has a nice cast-iron storefront and an engaging set of decorations along the cornice. What's most interesting about this building is that it currently contains an Italian social club where people of Italian ancestry gather to drink coffee, watch boxing matches and converse about current events.

6 Continue walking west along the north side of West Flournoy Street for approximately half a block. When you reach South Lytle Street, turn left and walk south to West Lexington Street. Turn right onto West Lexington Street and walk a few paces to 1246 West Lexington Street.

The John Coughlan House at 1246 West Lexington Street was built in 1871, when this area was largely populated by recent arrivals from Ireland. Like its neighbours at 1254–1262 West Lexington Street, the house was built in the Italianate style and all of these dwellings look out onto Arrigo Park across the street.

7 Walk west along Lexington Street for two blocks. At South Loomis Street turn left and walk south for two blocks to the intersection with West Taylor Street. Turn right onto West Taylor Street and walk 200ft (6m) or so along the south side of the street.

Tucked neatly on Taylor Street is this very pleasant piazza named after Joe DiMaggio, the American baseball star of the 1940s and 1950s. The piazza was finished in 1998, and it includes a series of benches, columns and a very prominent statue of the Yankee Clipper himself.

8 Cross over West Taylor Street to the National Italian American Sports Hall of Fame.

Designed to honour the many Italian Americans who have boxed, batted and swung their way to athletic prowess, the National Italian American Sports Hall of Fame entered these new digs in 2000. The collections include Rocky Marciano's heavyweight championship belt and swimming star Matt Biondi's various medals.

NATIONAL ITALIAN AMERICAN SPORTS HALL OF FAME;
www.niashf.org

9 Walk west along Taylor Street for three blocks. At South Paulina Street turn right and walk north for one block to West Polk Street. Turn left onto West Polk Street and walk a few paces to the CTA train station.

Millennium Park

This tour takes in Millennium Park and offers fantastic views of the architecture in the area and some spectacularly created public spaces.

In the park is an outdoor music pavilion designed by Frank Gehry (born 1929), a sculpture that takes its cues from liquid mercury and a water fountain that features the faces of 1,000 Chicagoans. The area that became today's Millennium Park was certainly not predestined for greatness, as anyone walking through in the 19th or most of the 20th century would point out. For much of that time, the area was used by the railways for various purposes, and it presented a rather unsightly counterpoint to the manicured grounds of the rest of Grant Park. In 1997, Mayor Daley began to have a series of epiphanies that would lead to the creation of Millennium Park. He had already begun thinking about placing planters in the middle of Chicago's broad and sometimes gloomy north to south boulevards, so why not work his vision into a new park? Several private partners were signed up (hence the corporate names that grace some of the elements), and seven years later the park opened to the public. Take time wandering as the park is a great place to spend a few hours just people-watching.

After leaving the CTA train station, walk east along East Randolph Street for a block to the corner of North Michigan Avenue and Randolph Street. Here on the southwest corner sits the Chicago Cultural Center.

The Chicago Cultural Center is housed in a building of great gravitas, and walking in through the main entrance makes one feel a bit of civic pride. It was originally built to house the central branch of the Chicago Public Library, and today it houses the main tourist information centre on the first floor. Pick up a few pieces of information and learn more about the city's free neighbourhood tours here. Walk through the building to the grand staircase near the Washington Street entrance and ascend to the third floor to take in the Tiffany dome in the Preston Bradley Hall and the expansive and elaborate decorations in the Grand Army of the Republic Memorial.

CHICAGO CULTURAL CENTER;
www.cityofchicago.org/Tourism/CulturalCenter

2 Walk out of the main entrance of the Chicago Cultural Center back onto Randolph Street. Turn right and cross North Michigan Avenue to enter Millennium Park. Once across the street walk for a few paces into the Wrigley Square and Millennium Monument.

Along with offering information about the donors who helped make Millennium Park possible, the Millennium Monument offers a nod to the lakefront park's past. The monument is probably a replica of

WHERE TO EAT

RUSSIAN TEA TIME,
77 East Adams Street;
Tel: 312-360-0000.
A cosy spot that is popular with the pre-theatre crowd. Specialties include a Ukrainian *borscht, pelmeni* (traditional Russian dumplings) and many beet-heavy dishes. $$

PARK GRILL,
11 North Michigan Avenue (on the east side of McCormick Tribune Plaza in Millennium Park);
Tel: 312-521-7275.
Traditional upmarket American cuisine (steaks, burgers and other meats) and the drinks list is quite inventive. Sit outside and watch the people pass by. $$$

GOLD COAST DOGS,
159 North Wabash Avenue;
Tel: 312-917-1677.
This establishment has served hot dogs to everyone from the common man to the occasional uncommon celebrity. $

the original peristyle that was located near the site from 1917 to 1953. It tends to be a bit quieter than the rest of the park, so think about sitting down here with a coffee for a break.

3 Walk north around the Millennium Monument back to Randolph Street and go east for about 100ft (30m) to the

DISTANCE **I mile (1.6km)**

ALLOW **2 hours**

START **CTA train station at East Randolph Street and North Wabash Avenue**

FINISH **CTA train station at East Madison Street and North Wabash Avenue**

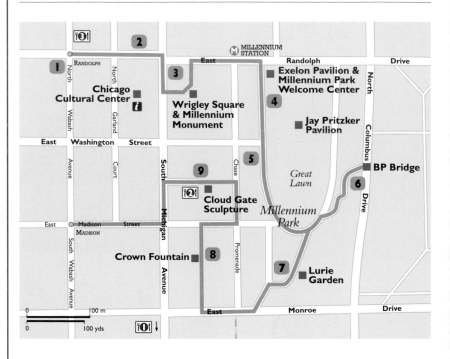

Exelon Pavilion and the Millennium Park Welcome Center.

So you're in front of a large black cube… what next, you ask? This black cube happens to be one of the four Exelon Pavilions, which happen to form part of Chicago's strategy regarding 'green' design. Located throughout the park, the pavilions convert solar energy into electricity. They add a bit of a 'Star Wars' flavour to the whole place, and they're good for the city's growing green image.

The Welcome Center is here at 201 East Randolph Street, and visitors can stop in to get more information about the park.

4 Walk south from the Exelon Pavilion for about 200ft (60m) or so, to the Jay Pritzker Pavilion.

It's hard to miss the intersecting and playful brushed stainless steel ribbons that create the Jay Pritzker Pavilion, and it's worth taking a minute to step back and take it all in. Designed by noted architect

OPPOSITE: CROWN FOUNTAIN, A CENTREPIECE IN MILLENNIUM PARK

Frank Gehry, the pavilion has two seating areas that can accommodate a total of 11,000 people. During the summer the Grant Park Symphony and Chorus holds court here and the concerts are delightfully offered free of charge.

5 Walk south around the pavilion and the Great Lawn (the grass seating area) and curve around until you reach the BP Bridge.

After leaving the Pritzker Pavilion you'll find yourself at the sinewy steel stylings of the BP Bridge, also a Frank Gehry creation. The bridge is clad in brushed stainless steel panels, and it winds its way across Columbus Drive. Walk across, pause for a breath and then walk back again.

6 After crossing back over the BP Bridge, walk a few paces to the south to reach the Lurie Garden.

Poet Robert Frost (1874–1963) is known for having taken the road less travelled, and this part of the tour allows you to take the path that goes through a part of Millennium Park that is a bit less travelled (but not by much). Walking down the so-called 'seam' pathway through the Lurie Garden will expose you to the indigenous prairie plant life that dominated the Chicago area before the days of the skyscraper, mass transit and other such urban features. Created by contemporary Dutch garden designer Piet Oudolf (born 1944), it contains over 1,800 native North American grasses. The

ABOVE: THE JAY PRITZKER PAVILION LOOKS STUNNING LIT UP AT NIGHT BY MAUVE LIGHTS

Jaume Plensa (born 1955), the Crown Fountain consists of two 50ft (15m) glass block towers placed at the end of a reflecting pool. Each fountain features a rotating cast of Chicagoans, and from mid-spring to mid-fall their mouths periodically burst forth with jets of water. It's a great sight, and in terms of people-watching the fountain is hard to beat.

8 Walk north past the fountain and after a close examination, walk east along the landscaped pedestrian walkway. Turn left onto the Chase Promenade, and left again to come face to face with the *Cloud Gate* sculpture.

Created by Turner Prize recipient Anish Kapoor (born 1954), the *Cloud Gate* sculpture weighs 100 tons and is 33ft (10m) high. Amazingly, the sculpture consists of a seamless series of polished steel plates. It reflects the surrounding skyline, and visitors flock to the underbelly of this floating 'bean' to take photographs of friends, family and complete strangers pictured in the concave surface. Kapoor was inspired by liquid mercury, and he has certainly proved himself up to the task of replicating this element in a form that is both seemingly static and yet full of motion and playfulness.

native plants used here provide a habitat for many bird species and they also attract helpful insects and butterflies.

7 After walking through the Lurie Garden, you will exit near East Monroe Drive. Turn right and walk west for about 200ft (60m), approaching the intersection of Monroe Street and South Michigan Avenue. Turn right before the intersection and walk north to the Crown Fountain.

During the summer, both children and adults play and gallivant around this fountain. About a thousand different faces are displayed on the fountain, lips pursed, just waiting to spout water every few minutes or so. Designed by Catalan artist

9 Walk west to Michigan Avenue and then turn left to walk south for a block. At East Madison Street, turn right to walk west back to the CTA station at the intersection with East Madison Street and North Wabash Avenue.

REFLECTING CHICAGO'S CITY LIGHTS AT NIGHT, THE ELLIPTICAL *CLOUD GATE* SCULPTURE

Under the Tracks and Back Again

Monk parakeets, grand hotels and the *pieds-à-terre* of legendary Chicago politicians are some of the attractions on this walk in East Hyde Park.

This area is more tranquil than the bustle of the commercial strip along 53rd Street on the other side of the tracks, and it's a good way to commune with Lake Michigan. The defining border of East Hyde Park is the elevated commuter rail track that whisks passengers to and from the Loop. The train was a boon to Hyde Park's development in the middle of the 19th century, and it continues to be an important link. In 1893 the World's Columbian Exposition came to Jackson Park, and this successful bazaar of cultures, technological wonders and old-fashioned entertainment transformed the area. Things kept moving in East Hyde Park during the 1910s and 1920s, as developers rushed in to build luxurious apartment buildings and hotels. A number of politicos have seen fit to ensconce themselves in the area, including the late Mayor Harold Washington (1922–87) and US Senator and presidential candidate Barack Obama (born 1961). Mayor Washington was a great defender of the displaced monk parakeets, which arrived here in the 1980s, and you'll hear them squawking about along the tour.

| Walk to the southeast corner of South Hyde Park Boulevard and East 53rd Street. Here stands the Del Prado Apartment building.

During the early decades of the 20th century, developers embarked on an ambitious programme of building hotels in East Hyde Park to accommodate visitors and tourists coming to the area. The Hotel Del Prado was one such building, and its lovely details include Native Americans rendered in terracotta and a heavily modified, yet still enjoyable, lobby space. For decades, it was also where the opponents of the Chicago White Sox baseball team stayed while they were batting and pitching out their differences at Comiskey Park.

2 Continue walking east along East 53rd Street for about 100ft (30m) as far as the Hampton House at the southwest corner of East 53rd Street and South East View Park.

Noted African-American politician and Chicago mayor Harold Washington made the Hampton House his home during his tenure in office, and blues legend Koko Taylor (born 1928) also resided here. Directly across the street is Harold Washington Park, which is probably the only park in Chicago with a sizeable monk parakeet population. Mayor Washington was quite a fan of these birds, and you only need to glance up to see their nests.

3 Turn south onto South East View Park and walk one block south to the southwest corner of East View Park and East 54th Street.

East View Park is an old-school gated community from the 1920s, and with

OPPOSITE: WALKING NEAR PROMONTORY POINT; ABOVE: HAROLD WASHINGTON PARK

DISTANCE **2.3 miles (3.7km)**

ALLOW **2.5 hours**

START **CTA bus stop at corner of East 53rd Street and South Hyde Park Blvd**

FINISH **Metra commuter rail station on East 57th Street**

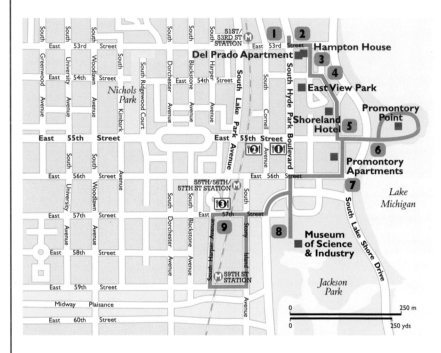

its elaborate guardhouse at the entrance, it gives off an air of Tudor-infused nobility. Today, it's a popular residence for professors, professionals and, until relatively recently, US Senator Barack Obama and his family.

4 Continue walking south for half a block on East View Park, which turns into South Lake Shore Drive. At this point, you will be standing in front of the Shoreland Hotel at 5454 South Lake Shore Drive.

Before it was pressed into service as an undergraduate dormitory for the University of Chicago, the Shoreland Hotel was a glamorous destination for Chicago's elite. With its two ballrooms, elaborate porte cochère (covered gateway) and sumptuous lobby, the hotel was well positioned next to Lake Michigan. A few years after its completion in 1926, Lake Shore Drive came roaring along in front, and the lakefront was a bit more distant in every sense of the phrase. Guests of

the hotel included Elvis Presley (1935–77), Jimmy Hoffa (1913–disappeared 1975) and the author of this volume, who was a student at the university during his four-year stay.

5 Turn east and cross over South Lake Shore Drive into the adjacent park. Walk a few paces to use the pedestrian underpass that provides safe passage underneath Lake Shore Drive. Here you will find a path that will loop around Promontory Point.

Promontory Point provides cinematic views of the Loop that often appear in major film releases. The Point was created as part of a massive federal works project in the 1930s, and it has remained immensely popular ever since. Running, jogging, sleeping and conversing are all popular daytime activities here. There have been plans to modify the Point in recent years, but they have met with strong resistance from community leaders, so it may be many more years before any action is taken.

6 After walking back underneath the pedestrian underpass, turn left onto South Lake Shore Drive. Walk south on South Lake Shore Drive until you reach the Promontory Apartments at 5530 South Lake Shore Drive.

This rather unassuming apartment building has the distinction of being Mies van der Rohe's first high rise. It was finished in 1949 and is on the National Register of Historic Places.

7 Continue walking south on South Lake Shore Drive to its intersection with East 56th Street. Turn right and walk two blocks west to the intersection of South Hyde Park

THE MUSEUM OF SCIENCE AND INDUSTRY, ORIGINALLY CONSTRUCTED AS THE PALACE OF FINE ARTS

Boulevard and East 56th Street. At this intersection, turn left to walk south on South Hyde Park Boulevard for two blocks. It is hard to miss the neoclassical Museum of Science and Industry building at this point.

Building the World's Columbian Exposition fairgrounds was a monumental undertaking, and the Palace of Fine Arts (now the Museum of Science and Industry) is the only remaining major structure from that most momentous event of 1893. The building was abandoned in the 1920s, and it was fortunately rebuilt in 1933 with monies provided by the city's park district and philanthropist Julius Rosenwald (1862–1932). Today you can visit the museum's German submarine, the U-505, look over a fully stocked miniature castle and take a ride through a demonstration coal mine.

MUSEUM OF SCIENCE AND INDUSTRY;
www.msichicago.org

8 Walk back north on South Hyde Park Boulevard to East 57th Street. Take a left and walk west on East 57th Street as it curves around the museum. Continue walking west on East 57th Street to South Stony Island Avenue. At South Stony Island Avenue and East 57th Street turn left and walk south to East 59th Street. At East 59th Street, turn right and walk underneath the commuter railroad tracks to South Harper Avenue. At South Harper Avenue, turn right and walk north until you reach East 57th Street.

WHERE TO EAT

|O| THE SNAIL,
1649 East 55th Street;
Tel: 773-667-5423.
This tiny Thai place in the heart of Hyde Park has good curry options, and the price is right. $

|O| THE NILE RESTAURANT,
1611 East 55th Street;
Tel: 773-324-9499.
The Nile Restaurant provides a taste of the Middle East; it does a mean hummus plate. $

|O| CAFFE FLORIAN,
1450 East 57th Street;
Tel: 773-752-4100.
With fun art on the walls, this spot has been a favourite among students and locals alike for years. The pizza takes top honours here. $

The stretch of South Harper Avenue from 57th to 59th Street is positively adorable. Developed in the late 19th century as a planned community called Rosalie Court, the street here is dominated by quirky houses with various turrets and playful architectural details. Exterior paints range from purple to yellow, and yawning cats are a hallmark of the many wide porches.

9 Turn right onto East 57th Street and continue a few paces more until you arrive at the commuter rail station to catch a ride home.

Grey Gothic Glories: University of Chicago

The lofty ideals and the equally lofty buildings of the University of Chicago campus are the focus on this tour through a great Chicago institution.

Along the way you will get to peek at a statue that marks the beginning of the Atomic Age, a grotesque-encrusted gate and the many neo-Gothic buildings. Hyde Park was on its way to becoming a place of prominence in the late 19th century, but the creation of the University of Chicago, along with the World's Columbian Exposition of 1893, really put Hyde Park on the map, in a manner of speaking. Retail-goods magnate Marshall Field (he of department-store fame) donated land for the University of Chicago's campus, and that very sober billionaire John D. Rockefeller (1839–1937) provided much of the initial money. The area for the new campus looked much like a typical Midwestern prairie before construction began in 1892, and the original plan designed for the campus's core provided for six quadrangles. As you wander around the campus today, you will notice that it has grown far beyond the Main Quadrangle.

1 After getting off the bus, cross west over South Ellis Avenue to the southwest corner of East 55th Street and Ellis Avenue.

Opened in the fall of 2003, the Gerald Ratner Athletics Center was the first new athletic facility built on the University of Chicago campus in almost 70 years. For the first four decades of its existence, the university was a perennial powerhouse in collegiate sports. Robert Maynard Hutchins (1899–1977), the university's president, decided to remove the pernicious influence of college sports from the university milieu in the 1930s, and the school withdrew from the Big Ten conference in 1946. Designed by architect César Pelli (born 1926), the Athletics Center signifies a renewed commitment to sporting life on campus. All told, the building contains an Olympic-sized swimming pool, basketball courts and a wide range of exercise equipment. Take a look at the trophy display directly inside the main entrance that recounts the glory days of sports at the university.

WHERE TO EAT

|O| DIVINITY SCHOOL
COFFEE SHOP,
1025 East 58th Street (in the basement of Swift Hall, University of Chicago's Main Quadrangle);
Tel: 773-702-4806.
Scholars, students and visitors alike enjoy the salads, Thai food and other local offerings at this campus favourite. $

|O| MEDICI ON 57TH STREET,
1327 East 57th Street;
Tel: 773-667-7394.
Hyde Park's college hangout offers up good breakfasts surrounded by local art and served on tables that have been carved up with thousands of initials and various engravings. $

|O| NOODLES, ETC.,
1333 East 57th Street;
Tel: 773-684-2801.
A basic noodle shop that bustles with students. $

2 Cross back over South Ellis Avenue and continue south on Ellis Avenue for one block to the southeast corner of Ellis Avenue and East 56th Street. Here you can hardly mistake the Max Palavesky Residential Commons.

This explosion of colour might seem to be straight out of sunny Spain, but it's actually a playful bit of architectural exposition by noted Mexican architect Ricardo Legoretta (born 1931). The building in question here houses over 700 undergraduates at the university. When it was completed in 2001, a handful of neighbours complained that the purple and orange deployed around the building's edges made it look like something from *Sesame Street*.

3 Continue walking south for about 20 paces until you reach the Henry

DISTANCE **1.75 miles (2.8km)**

ALLOW **2 hours**

START **CTA bus stop at East 55th Street and South Ellis Avenue**

FINISH **Metra commuter rail station on East 59th Street**

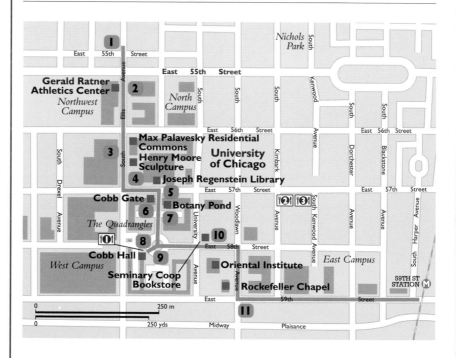

Moore sculpture immediately south of the Max Palavesky Residential Commons.

Cast from bronze, this abstract sculpture by the English artist Henry Moore (1898–1986) was placed on the site to commemorate the 25th anniversary of the first self-sustaining, controlled nuclear chain reaction in 1942. The reaction took place on the site (which was then located underneath some squash courts), and was conducted by the Nobel Prize recipient Professor Enrico Fermi (1901–54) and his colleagues. Frequently visited by peace organizations and tour buses, the site is a testimony to both the inherent possibilities and the dangers created by the birth of the atomic age. A small model of the sculpture resides in the Tate Modern in London.

4 Continue walking south to the corner of East 57th Street and South Ellis Avenue. Staying on the north side of East 57th Street, turn left and walk east to the middle of the block.

Although we still haven't made it to the grey Gothic heart of the University of Chicago's campus, the seven-storey Joseph Regenstein Library does offer a substantial bit of grey. With its very over-the-top brutalism, it is but a mere taste of what modernist architect Walter Netsch, Jr. (1920–2008) brought to his designs on the University of Illinois at Chicago campus in the 1960s. Joseph Regenstein (1899–1957) was a rather interesting Chicago industrialist, as he made much of his fortune through his most popular invention, the window envelope.

5 Turn around and use the crossing (crossway) in front of the library to the south side of East 57th Street.

Its grotesques and lovely carvings distinguish Cobb Gate as the north entrance to the main quadrangles of the university, which was designed in 1897 by the university's first architect and planner, Henry Ives Cobb (1859–1931). Today, campus guides comment that each grotesque represents a year in the life of the average undergraduate. This may be the reason that the grotesque at the top of Cobb Gate appears a bit triumphant, if not exhausted.

6 Walk south underneath Cobb Gate for about 10 paces.

Graduating classes from the University of Chicago have offered up various gifts over the past century or so, the most lovely of which is perhaps Botany Pond. During the spring and summer months,

you will see turtles and fish swimming around, and there are several benches that provide a place to rest. The bridge that passes over the pond was a gift from the graduating class of 1922.

7 Continue walking south for about 30 paces until reaching the middle of the roundabout (traffic circle) at the centre of the Main Quadrangle.

Stopping here is a great way to take in the heart of the grey Gothic campus of the University of Chicago and the lovely landscaping that is an integral part of the campus. The campus was designated an official botanical garden in 1997 by the American Association of Botanical Gardens and Arboreta. In one glance here, you can take in some of the campus's impressive elms and the regional plantings that include hollies, yew hedges and hawthorns. To learn more about the campus and university, consult the website. **UNIVERSITY OF CHICAGO;**

www.uchicago.edu/

8 Walk southwest along the diagonal path that leads away from the traffic circle for about 20 paces.

When the University of Chicago opened in 1892, Cobb Hall was the only completed building on campus. At the time, it housed all of the university's administrative offices, classrooms and lecture halls. Architect Henry Ives Cobb replicated its Gothic style across much of the Main Quadrangle. Today it houses classrooms and the Renaissance Society (located on the fourth floor), which displays a wide range of modern art.

9 Turn around and walk northeast for about 20 paces to the centre of the roundabout. At the roundabout, turn right and walk east along East 58th Street to the corner of East 58th Street and South University Avenue.

On the northeast corner of this intersection stands the most excellent Seminary Coop Bookstore. It is housed in the basement of the Chicago Theological Seminary, and bibliophiles should definitely stop off here. Across the street is the Oriental Institute, a research establishment that contains a museum dedicated to the art, history and archaeology of ancient Egypt, Nubia and Persia. The museum displays objects recovered by Oriental Institute excavations in permanent galleries, as well as rotating exhibitions.

ORIENTAL INSTITUTE;

http://oi.uchicago.edu/museum/

10 Continue walking east on East 58th Street for one block to the corner of East 58th Street and South Woodlawn Avenue. At this intersection, turn south to reach the Rockefeller Chapel, on the corner of East 59th Street and Woodlawn Avenue.

Arches and buttresses abound on this high-flying neo-Gothic church designed by Bertram Goodhue (1869–1924). The chapel, completed in 1928, is the central gathering point for many major functions at the University of Chicago, including graduation ceremonies, receptions for international guests of distinction and choral concerts. The building was initially called University Chapel, but the name was changed to honour the university's founder, John D. Rockefeller.

11 Continue walking east down East 59th Street for four blocks and eventually you will reach the Metra commuter rail station at East 59th Street and South Harper Avenue.

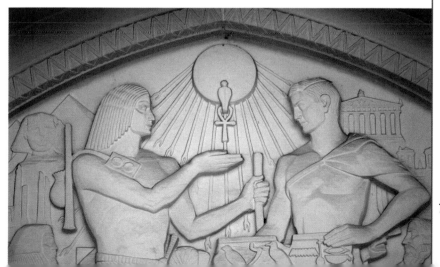

THE MODERN SIDE OF THE UNIVERSITY OF CHICAGO CAMPUS

Pullman: Sleeping Cars, Restless Workers

Visit one of the United States' best-known planned communities of the 19th century, today an official city of Chicago landmark district.

George Pullman (1831-97) developed the railroad sleeping car to help ease the journeys of long-distance passengers, marketed as 'luxury for the middle class'. In 1880, Pullman began construction of his new town next to the Illinois Central Railroad right-of-way. Pullman enlisted the help of architect Solon S. Beman (1853–1914) to create a town that would contain adequate housing for his factory workers, a hotel, a market place and a town plaza. Workers at the factory rented their homes from the company, bought their goods from the company store, and so on. This worked well until the depression that rolled across the US in 1893. Rents in Pullman remained steep, while wages were cut. Workers were fed up with Pullman's heavy-handed paternalism, and in 1894 there was a general strike. The US Army was called in to break up the strike and, for a time, Pullman was one of the most hated men in America. Courts forced the company to divest its ownership in the town and buildings were sold to private owners.

I After leaving the Metra train station at 111th Street, walk east along East 111th Street for two blocks to the intersection of East 111th Street and South Forrestville Avenue. Turn right and walk 10 paces to the south.

Built in 1881 at a cost of one million dollars, George Pullman named this hotel at the centre of his 'perfect town' after his favourite daughter, Florence. The original portion of the hotel contained 50 well-appointed guest rooms, a dining room, billiard room, barber shop and the only bar in this company town. The building originally had gas lights and was heated with steam radiators generated by the Corliss engine in the factory across the street. Today the building is undergoing major renovation and is closed to the public, but you can call ahead (tel: 773-660-2341) to arrange entrance to the building.

2 Walk south to the intersection of East 111th Place and South Forrestville Avenue. Turn left onto East 111th Place and walk east half a block to the intersection of East 111th Place and South Saint Lawrence Avenue. Cross over to the east side of South Saint Lawrence Avenue and continue walking south for about 10 paces.

The terraced (row) houses that stretch from 11145 to 11151 South Saint Lawrence Avenue were built to house George Pullman's factory workers. In fact, they were the first houses to be built for the new company town in 1880, and

WHERE TO EAT

🍽 PULLMAN'S PUB,
611 East 113th Street;
Tel: 773-568-0264.
This place is as down-home as it gets, and it offers a very basic set of beers and spirits. $

🍽 CAL-HARBOR RESTAURANT & LOUNGE,
546 East 115th Street;
Tel: 773-264-5435.
A true Chicago-style breakfast spot that piles on the corned beef hash and pancakes. $

🍽 ARTHUR'S BARB-B-Q,
335 East 115th Street;
Tel: 773-821-4558.
Standard BBQ fare, including ribs and French fries. Cash only and it's closed on Sunday. $

they continue to be an affordable housing option for those looking to move into the neighbourhood.

3 Continue walking south along the east side of South Saint Lawrence Avenue to the intersection of East 112th Street and South Saint Lawrence. On the southeast corner of this intersection you will see the Greenstone United Methodist Church.

This church is appropriately named, as it was built of a very green serpentine stone imported from a quarry in New England.

DISTANCE 2 miles (3.2km)

ALLOW 2 hours

START Metra commuter rail station on East 111th Street

FINISH Metra commuter rail station on East 111th Street

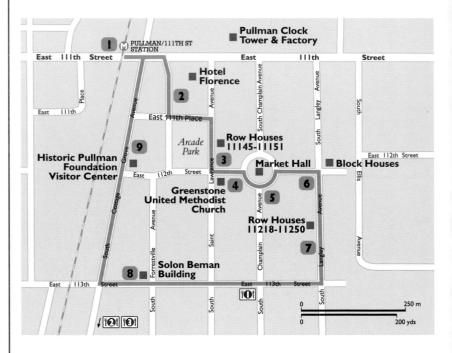

Finished in 1882, the church was first established as a place for all Christian denominations, but due to the high costs associated with using the facility, a number of religious groups opted to meet elsewhere in the town. Today the church houses a Methodist congregation, which has been here since 1907.

4 Walk one block east along East 112th Street to the Market Hall at the intersection of East 112th Street and South Champlain Avenue.

Pullman town planner Solon S. Beman inserted this slice of Italian urban design and architecture quite nicely into the fabric of the growing company town in 1892. The existing colonnaded apartment buildings around the Market Hall featured both stores and apartments, and the central structure in the market provided fresh produce and meats. The city of Chicago is currently working towards adding new landscaping and lighting to this area to improve its general appearance and feel.

OPPOSITE: PULLMAN'S HOTEL FLORENCE, AT THE CENTRE OF THE PLANNED COMMUNITY

5 Walk around the Market Hall and continue east along East 112th Street for one block to the corner of East 112th Street and South Langley Avenue. Cross over to the northeast corner of this intersection.

In other parts of Chicago, these rather simple brick buildings would be called tenements, but in Pullman they were known as blockhouses. They were built for common labourers working in the nearby Pullman factories, and they continue to house two-bedroom apartments to this day.

6 Cross back over to the west side of South Langley Avenue and walk south on Langley Avenue for 20 paces.

Packed in alongside other similar structures, the simple, yet varied façades

ABOVE: A RAILCAR UNDER CONSTRUCTION AT THE PULLMAN FACTORY

of the terraced (row) houses between 11218 and 11250 South Langley Avenue offer a taste of the architectural variations that can be created with a bit of ingenuity and playfulness. As you pass by you will notice the mix of awnings, bay windows, dormer windows and the materials used such as limestone and dark-coloured bricks that contribute to the individual flavour of each dwelling.

7 Walk south to the corner of South Langley Avenue and East 113th Street. At 113th Street, turn right and walk three blocks west to the northwest corner of East 113th Street and South Forrestville Avenue.

This rather square corner building was an unusual variation offered up by Solon Beman—note the high mansard roof—and you will see several other examples of this building type along East 113th Street.

8 Walk west along East 113th Street for one block to the intersection of East 113th Street and South Cottage Grove Avenue. Turn right and walk one block north on Cottage Grove Avenue to the corner of East 112th Street and Cottage Grove Avenue. Continue for about 20 paces to the Historic Pullman Foundation Visitor Center.

After walking around Pullman, the Pullman Visitor Center is a good place to stop and take in a few exhibits on the history of the area and watch a 20-minute introductory film about the creation and development of the community. Check out the website for more information.

HISTORIC PULLMAN FOUNDATION;
www.pullmanil.org

9 When you leave the visitor centre walk north on South Cottage Grove for two blocks until reaching East 111th Street. Turn left and proceed back to the Metra commuter rail station.

Lions, Miró, Chagall: Sculpture in the Loop

The Loop has been an exciting place to view public art for over a century; admire a colourful mosaic by Marc Chagall or the towering work of Picasso.

The other works of art featured on this tour include Joan Miró's abstract sculpture *Miss Chicago* across the street from the Picasso and the very lifelike bronze lions that guard the Impressionist masterpieces of the Art Institute of Chicago. The history of public art in the Loop goes back to the late 19th century when the Art Institute of Chicago began to offer up a number of works in public spaces for the enjoyment and edification of the general public. The works tended to be quite traditional in their subject matter (great men, great explorers, city founders and so on) for many decades. After a quiet period on the art front, new public art installations began popping up in the late 1960s and early 1970s, in places such as Daley Plaza and the new federal building complex along Dearborn Street. A boost to these public art programmes continued with the creation of the city's Percent-for-Art Ordinance in 1978. The ordinance dictated that a percentage of the cost of construction and renovation of municipal buildings must be set aside for the acquisition of artworks for these buildings.

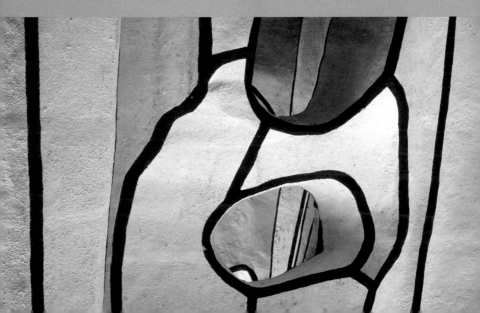

1 After exiting the CTA station onto West Lake Street, walk east to the intersection of West Lake Street and North Clark Street. Stay on the west side of North Clark Street and continue one block south to the northwest corner of West Randolph Street and North Clark Street.

French artist and sculptor Jean Dubuffet (1901–85) created this rather striking piece of public art shortly before he died in 1985. The 29ft (9m) high fibreglass work is titled *Monument with Standing Beast* and it features four elements that are meant to suggest a standing animal, a portal, a tree and an abstract architectural form. It's hard to miss the rather large spaceship-like building that provides a dramatic backdrop for the work: it happens to be the James R. Thompson Center, designed by Helmut Jahn (born 1940).

2 Walk east along West Randolph Street for one block to the intersection of West Randolph Street and North Dearborn Street. Turn right onto North Dearborn Street and walk south for about 25 paces. Turn right and walk a few steps into the Daley Civic Center Plaza.

This 50ft (15m) high sculpture by Pablo Picasso (1881–1973) was placed in Daley Plaza in 1967 and it's been a source of controversy and enjoyment for over four decades. Prior to that, there hadn't been much new public art placed in the city's Loop for decades, and this work represented a radical break with the more traditional heroic style sculptures that were par for the public art course before then. Emissaries from the city visited Picasso and gave him a few items related to the city's history such as old postcards and books, and he set himself to the task of creating a new work. The final piece was assembled in the United States Steel factory in Gary, Indiana, and made its way to the Loop. Picasso never said explicitly what the work was meant to resemble, though it did upset a number of more traditional folks with its abstract qualities. One city politician even suggested that the work be replaced with a statue of a famous baseball player.

3 Walk south across Daley Plaza to the intersection of North Dearborn Street and West Washington Street.

DISTANCE 2 miles (3.2km)

ALLOW 2.5 hours

START CTA train station on West Lake Street

FINISH CTA train station on East Adams Street

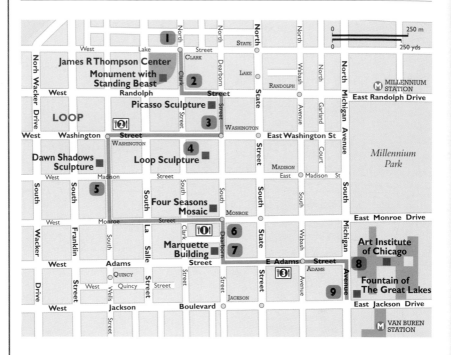

Cross over Washington Street and turn right to walk about 30 paces west on Washington Street.

Joan Miró (1893–1983) was particularly fond of Chicago, hence he donated the design of this unusual sculpture to the city. The various forms in this 39ft (12m) high work reference an earth deity, a star and rays of light. Constructed of steel, wire mesh, concrete, bronze and ceramic tile, the sculpture was installed on this site in 1981.

4 Continue walking west along the south side of West Washington Street for three blocks to North Wells Street (hard to miss as the elevated train rumbles overhead). Turn south onto North Wells Street and walk south one block to the northwest corner of West Madison Street and North Wells Street.

Born in Kiev, Russia, Louise Nevelson (1899–1988) was known for her creative assemblages that frequently brought together a variety of forms.

OPPOSITE: JOAN MIRÓ'S *MISS CHICAGO* SCULPTURE IN THE BRUNSWICK PLAZA ON WASHINGTON STREET

This sculpture entitled *Dawn Shadows* was inspired by the nearby elevated train and is constructed of steel, painted in her signature colour, matte black. It's good to walk all around this sculpture to appreciate it fully, and one of the best vantage points happens to be the elevated train station across the street.

5 Walk south along Wells Street to the corner of Wells Street and West Monroe Street. Turn left on to West Monroe Street and continue three blocks east to the northwest corner of West Monroe Street and South

Dearborn Street. Walk down into the sunken Bank One Plaza.

Marc Chagall (1897–1985) was a master of many media, and this 70ft (21m) long, 14ft (4m) high, 10ft (3m) wide rectangular box features his masterful mosaic *Four Seasons*. The mosaic is comprised of thousands of inlaid chips in over 250 colours, and you will note the presence of suns, fish, birds and one of Chagall's favourite tropes, a pair of lovers. The mosaic also incorporates different images from Chicago's dramatic skyline, and Chagall continued to modify the design after its arrival in the Windy City.

6 Walk back out of the plaza and continue south on South Dearborn Street for one block to the northwest corner of West Adams Street and South Dearborn Street.

The Marquette Building at this busy corner is a landmark in its own right, built by the distinguished firm of Holabird & Roche between 1893 and 1895. Its brick and terracotta cladding make it stand out from its neighbours, and the bronze sculptures along the Dearborn Street side are mini-masterpieces depicting the travels of noted missionary and explorer Father Jacques Marquette (1637–76). The bronze bas-reliefs were executed by Hermon Atkins MacNeil (1866–1947) and include scenes from Marquette's travels in the late 17th century into 'strange lands', which of course included the area that became Chicago. Step inside the

ABOVE: ONE OF TWO BRONZE LIONS GUARDING THE ENTRANCE TO THE ART INSTITUTE OF CHICAGO

building during business hours to take in the additional mosaics that depict even more scenes of French exploration and the bronze relief sculptures of various Native American leaders.

7 Walk east along East Adams Street for three blocks to its intersection with South Michigan Avenue. Navigate the pedestrian crossing (crossway) to get to the east side of Michigan Avenue.

Standing watch over the Art Institute of Chicago are two bronze lions created by sculptor Edward L. Kemeys (1843–1907). The lions have been there since 1894 and they are periodically decked out in the regalia of Chicago's professional sports teams; during the holidays they will have wreaths placed around their necks. The building behind them isn't too shabby either, as it houses one of the world's premier art museums. Built in 1893 by the architectural firm of Shepley, Rutan & Coolidge, the neoclassical structure conveys a Gilded-Age sense of importance and permanence. It also happens to have a few very important works of art inside.

ART INSTITUTE OF CHICAGO;
www.artic.edu/aic

8 Walk south about 20 paces along Michigan Avenue. Here you will find the entrance to the Art Institute's South Garden and inside is the Fountain of the Great Lakes.

This fountain by Lorado Taft (1860–1936) was created between 1907 and

WHERE TO EAT

🍴 ITALIAN VILLAGE,
71 West Monroe Street;
Tel: 312-332-7005.
Three Italian restaurants stacked on top of each other, with standard fare but a pleasant atmosphere. **$$**

🍴 HANNAH'S BRETZEL,
180 West Washington Street;
Tel: 312-621-1111.
Organic everything rules the day here, including whole-grain soups, coffee and sandwiches. **$**

🍴 RHAPSODY RESTAURANT,
65 East Adams Street;
Tel: 312-786-9911.
Within the Symphony Center, this upmarket restaurant features everything from risotto to *mahi-mahi*. **$$$**

1913 and depicts five women who are meant to represent the five Great Lakes: Superior, Michigan, Huron, Erie and Ontario. Taft was an instructor at the Art Institute of Chicago for many years, and his works grace other public spaces in the city, including his massive Fountain of Time along the Midway Plaisance in Hyde Park.

9 Return to South Michigan Avenue and walk north back to East Adams Street. Turn left onto East Adams Street and continue one block west to reach the CTA train station.

MARC CHAGALL'S *FOUR SEASONS* MOSAIC AT BANK ONE PLAZA

All Roads Lead to Uptown

Explore the past and present of Uptown's 'bright-lights' district, replete with late-night bars and ornately decorated movie theatres.

This area used to be known as the township of Lake View before being annexed to the city of Chicago in 1889. For much of the late 19th century the area was full of small farms and it was the centre of the Midwest's greenhouse industry. The arrival of elevated trains around 1900 quickened the pace of urbanization, and wherever two major streets met there was sure to be a bustling commercial district. One such intersection was at North Broadway and West Lawrence Avenue, in the heart of what was (and is) called the Uptown neighbourhood. It was also one of Chicago's most famous 'bright-lights' districts replete with late-night bars and ornately decorated movie theatres. In the post-war period things changed within Uptown as many people began to leave for the growing suburbs. In their wake, they left room for new arrivals from places like Appalachia and East Asia, who bolstered the retail area along Argyle Street even while the community began to suffer greatly from blight and abandonment.

Before leaving the CTA train station at Montrose, walk down from the platform and take a peek at the public art (see below) before passing out through the turnstiles.

The Montrose station was renovated by the Chicago Transit Authority (CTA) from 2006 to 2007 after 99 years of solid service (and relatively little maintenance). Along with making the station accessible to the handicapped, the CTA also installed some modern art by contemporary designer Jason Pickleman. The back wall of the station's interior now features street names in the Ravenswood and Uptown communities spelled out in thin metal sans-serif letters. Not a bad way to familiarize yourself with the local street names before setting out!

2 Walk east along West Montrose Avenue for a block and a half to the intersection of West Montrose Avenue and North Hermitage Avenue. Turn left onto the west side of North Hermitage Avenue and walk north for two blocks to the southwest corner of West Wilson Avenue and North Hermitage Avenue.

The Stick Style of architecture was all the rage between the 1860s and the 1890s, and All Saints' Episcopal Church is an excellent example of this rather unusual style. The sticks in question are actually flat boards applied to the exterior of the façade in a variety of geometric patterns. This 1883 church has such details in spades, and it also happens to be where noted poet Carl Sandburg

WHERE TO EAT

🍽 **GREEN MILL COCKTAIL LOUNGE,**
4802 North Broadway Avenue;
Tel: 773-878-5552.
Jazz, gin gimlets and poetry slams; a line-up which is hard to beat. $

🍽 **PHO 777,**
1065 West Argyle Street;
Tel: 773-561-9909.
As its name implies, *pho* (Vietnamese noodle soup) is the focus here, and favourites include chicken and basil *pho*, along with their brisket. $

🍽 **FIESTA MEXICANA,**
4806 North Broadway Avenue;
Tel: 773-769-4244.
Late-night dining can be a real treat here, as the low-cost Mexican fare is usually accompanied by Tejano pop music. $

(1878–1967) worshipped when he lived a little further up the street.

3 Cross north over West Wilson Avenue and walk east back over North Hermitage Street to the northeast corner of West Wilson Street and North Hermitage Street.

This prominent Queen Anne-style house is distinguished both by its fine wrap-around porch and its notable turret. From 1891 to 1921 it was the home of Dr Wallace C. Abbott (1857–1921), the

93

DISTANCE **2 miles (3.2km)**

ALLOW **2 hours**

START **CTA train station on West Montrose Avenue**

FINISH **CTA train station on West Lawrence Avenue**

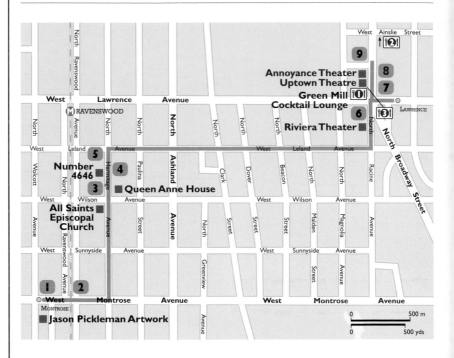

founder of Abbott Laboratories, which today employs over 65,000 people across every sector of health care.

4 Cross west back over North Hermitage Avenue and continue north on the west side of Hermitage for around 30 paces to 4646 North Hermitage Avenue.

Poet and author Carl Sandburg came to Chicago in 1912 to live on the second floor of this apartment building with his wife and young daughter. It was here that he penned the poem *Chicago*, which begins 'Hog butcher for the world/ tool maker, stacker of wheat'. Sandburg went on to win many literary accolades, including one Pulitzer Prize for his biography of Abraham Lincoln and another for his collected poems.

5 Walk north a few paces to West Leland Avenue. Turn right onto West Leland Avenue and walk east nine blocks to the intersection of North Racine

Avenue and West Leland Avenue.
Turn left onto the west side of North
Racine Avenue and walk north for
one block to the gleaming neon sign
of the famous Riviera Theater.

Back in the Jazz Age, this was one of
Chicago's finest places to take in a movie.
In those days visitors could leave their
children in a playroom and slip into a
velvet-covered chair to watch a show
or three. With the declining fortunes of
Uptown in the later 20th century (and
the movie-going business), the theatre
was transformed into a live music venue,
so take a look at the programme of
events if you're up for a show.

RIVIERA THEATER;

www.jamusa.com

6 Continue walking north 10 paces
or so to the corner of North
Broadway Street and West Lawrence
Avenue. Cross north over West
Lawrence Avenue. After a few steps
look for the neon sign that proclaims
'Green Mill Cocktail Lounge'.

Much of Chicago's rousing gangland past
has been bulldozed over and consigned
to the landfill heap of sordid history. The
Green Mill Cocktail Lounge, however, is
one part of that history that still survives.
This particular incarnation of the Green
Mill was opened in 1914 and by the
early 1920s it was partially owned by one
of Al Capone's cronies and henchman,
'Machine Gun' Jack McGurn (1905–36).
McGurn later met a violent end, which
surprised no one, but fortunately, the

music continued on. If you like jazz or
poetry slams, the Green Mill is a place
you must visit.

GREEN MILL COCKTAIL LOUNGE;

www.greenmilljazz.com

7 Continue walking about five
paces north on North Broadway
to the Uptown Theatre

When it was finished in 1925, the
Uptown Theatre was the largest theatre
in Chicago with almost 4,500 seats. Built
by legendary movie theatre architects
Rapp and Rapp, the exterior features
a fascinating mix of Spanish Baroque

elements, including elaborate stucco shells and garlands. The building has been largely vacant since 1981, though a dedicated volunteer organization is working on raising funds to restore the building to its former glory.

UPTOWN THEATRE;

www.uptowntheatre.com

8 Walk another five paces north to the Annoyance Theater at 4830 North Broadway.

The Annoyance Theater has been part of Chicago's highly regarded improvisational comedy scene since 1987, and is known for such works as *Co-ed Prison Sluts* and more recent shows like *Chicagoland*. Taking in a show here is a good bet, although some of the shows might not be 'family-friendly' in the strictest sense of the phrase.

ANNOYANCE THEATER;

www.theannoyance.com

9 Turn around and walk back south to the intersection of Broadway and Lawrence. Cross east over North Broadway and then walk south across West Lawrence Avenue. Walk east along West Lawrence Avenue for about 20 paces to the CTA train station.

ALAN GRESIK SWING SHIFT ORCHESTRA PLAYS AT THE GREEN MILL COCKTAIL LOUNGE

Wicker Park: Ethnic and Literary Heritage

On this walk, get a taste of Polish food, gritty Chicago literary realism and grandiose 19th-century homes—all important features of Wicker Park.

In Polonia Square, you'll find yourself surrounded by reminders of the area's long-standing Polish heritage. Moving down West Division Street, you will see shades of Wicker Park's contemporary ethnic mix in the small Polish shops and Mexican taquerias that sit side by side along the street. Noted author and oral historian Studs Terkel (born 1912) wrote about the experiences of Chicagoans in his book *Division Street: America*. While the book is not explicitly about people who live or work along Division Street, it's not hard to imagine the stories of the people going up and down the sidewalk here. The tour passes through the centre of Wicker Park, taking in mansions built by European immigrants who were willing to spend their hard-earned fortunes on buildings that symbolized their middle- and upper-class aspirations. You also get a taste of the hipster culture that has come to dominate Wicker Park in recent years.

After climbing out of the CTA's Division Street station (which is underground), walk over to Polonia Triangle. It's hard to miss as it sits in the middle of the intersection where North Ashland, North Milwaukee and West Division converge.

Despite its worn-down appearance today, this small park is an important site as it marks the historic heart of Chicago's large Polish community. Within a pierogi's throw (a pierogi being a Polish stuffed dumpling) of Polonia Triangle, one could once see the headquarters of the Polish National Alliance and the *Polish Daily News*. Both organizations have since decamped for other parts of the city, but the Polish flavour of the area lives on through such institutions as the Chopin Theatre and the Podhalanka restaurant, which are across the way on Division Street. The fountain at the centre of the park is named after noted Chicagoan and chronicler of the down-and-out Nelson Algren (1909–81), who lived nearby for many years.

2 Cross south over West Division Street and turn left onto Division Street. Walk about five paces to the Chopin Theatre.

Built in 1918 to serve Chicago's rapidly growing Polish population, the Chopin Theatre has been a centre of avant-garde cultural activity since it reopened in 1990. Since then, the theatre has been the home for events sponsored by the Chicago Filmmakers, Young Chicago

WHERE TO EAT

[O] **ESTELLE'S,**
2013 West North Avenue;
Tel: 773-782-0450.
Cheap beer and reasonably priced imports make for a diverse crowd at this bar suspiciously close to the elevated train line. $

[2] **PODHALANKA,**
1549 West Division Street;
Tel: 773-486-6655.
Pictures of Pope John Paul II and upcoming Polish-themed events adorn the walls of this no-frills pierogi-heavy eatery. $

[3] **MIRAI SUSHI,**
2020 West Division Street;
Tel: 773-862-8500.
Trendy sushi joint with a minimalist interior and a heavy dose of hipsters. $$$

Authors and the Chicago International Documentary Film Festival.
CHOPIN THEATRE;
www.chopintheatre.com

3 Turn around and walk west on West Division Street for six blocks. Cross over to the north side of West Division Street and walk across North Wolcott Street. After walking west along the north side of West Division Street for about 10 paces, you'll reach the Division Street Baths at 1914–1916 West Division Street.

99

DISTANCE **1.8 miles (2.9km)**

ALLOW **1.5 hours**

START **CTA train station on West Division Street**

FINISH **CTA train station on West North Avenue**

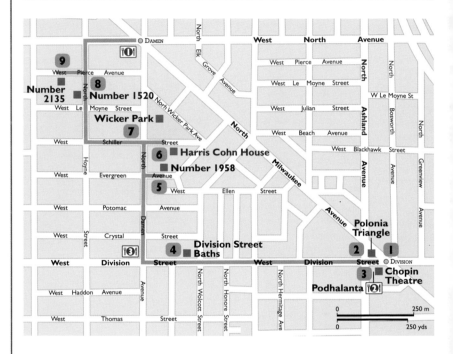

The authors Saul Bellow (1915–2005) and Nelson Algren used the baths at this traditional Russian bathhouse, which is the only one of its kind left in Chicago. Curious visitors can sample the cold pool, the warm pool and a eucalyptus-scented bath. It wouldn't be a bathhouse without a Russian *banya* (hot room), and they have one of these on the premises for patrons.

4 Continue walking west on West Division Street for one block to the intersection of West Division and North Damen Avenue. Turn right onto North Damen Avenue and walk three blocks north to West Evergreen Avenue. Turn right to walk on the north side of West Evergreen Avenue and proceed to 1958 West Evergreen Avenue.

Nelson Algren lived and breathed Chicago for much of his life, and he worked to chronicle the seedy underbelly that many would rather have forgotten in novels such as *The Man with the Golden*

OPPOSITE: FILTER COFFEE SHOP ON NEAR WEST SIDE OF WICKER PARK

Arm, Never Come Morning, A Walk on the Wild Side and Chicago: City on the Make. He lived here from 1959 to 1975 and a plaque in front of the building reads 'Lyrical, tough, tender, compassionate, he showed the people's pain'.

5 Turn around and walk west on West Evergreen Avenue back to its intersection with North Damen Avenue. Turn right to walk north on Damen Avenue for one block to West Schiller Street. Turn right onto West Schiller Street and walk about 10 paces to 1941 West Schiller Street.

Wicker Park is sometimes referred to as Chicago's ethnic Gold Coast as many well-off immigrants from Europe often elected to build large homes and mansions close to each other here. The

Harris Cohn house at 1941 West Schiller is just one example of such a house, distinguished by its prominent stone façade and its fine granite columns.

6 Retrace your steps along West Schiller Street to the northeast corner of Schiller Street and North Damen Avenue.

Charles G. and Joel H. Wicker were savvy businessmen and they knew that a park would be a great way to increase the value of property in their new development. They donated this small triangular parcel of land to Chicago in 1870, and their largesse paid off, as Wicker Park became a fashionable area for upwardly-mobile immigrants. Today Wicker Park includes a water playground and baseball fields.

7 Walk west on West Schiller for one block to the intersection of North Hoyne Street and West Schiller. Turn right on to North Hoyne Street and walk north one block to West Le Moyne Street. Cross over to the west side of Hoyne Street and continue walking north about 10 paces to 1520 North Hoyne Street.

The procession of elaborate homes continues on Hoyne Street as indicated by the bold Second Empire-style house built at this address in 1886. Look up to see the carved stylized portrait of a woman of the period.

8 Continue walking north on Hoyne Street to West Pierce Avenue. Then walk west on the south side of Pierce Avenue for around 20 paces to 2135 West Pierce Avenue.

This house, built for local furniture merchant Hermann Weinhardt in 1889, really takes the cake, which seems appropriate as it resembles a wooden cake redolent with architectural details such as carvings along the cornice line and the side porch with a garden view.

9 Walk east back on West Pierce Avenue and join the intersection of West Pierce and North Hoyne Street. Turn to the left and walk north on Hoyne Street for one block to its intersection with West North Avenue. Turn right onto West North Avenue and continue east one block until you reach the CTA station.

ACTION FROM WRIGLEY FIELD, HOME OF THE CHICAGO CUBS BASEBALL TEAM

Lakeview: A Synagogue, Some Salvation and Sport

A tour of Lakeview should always include what is arguably America's most fabled ballpark, Wrigley Field, home to the Chicago Cubs.

In the 19th century the area known as Lakeview was a pleasant place to farm and escape from some of the less charming aspects of Chicago, such as poor sanitation and a continuous 24-hour cacophony of noise. The township of Lakeview was annexed to the city proper in 1889, and change came quite rapidly after that. The elevated train reached as far north as Wilson Avenue by the turn of the century, and other major developments soon followed, including hundreds of small apartment buildings and the construction of Wrigley Field (then known as Weegham Park) in 1914. Today the area is immensely popular with young urbanites, and it also has a very visible GLBT (gay, lesbian, bisexual and transgender) community. This tour may be a little more difficult to complete when the Cubs are playing at Wrigley Field, but if you turn a blind eye to a few inebriated hooligans, you'll be just fine. You will also get a chance to visit the Byzantine-styled Temple Sholom and catch a glimpse of the walled compound owned by the Salvation Army.

I
After hopping off the train at the CTA's Addison stop, walk down the stairs, keeping tabs on the murals by artist Steve Musgrave (born 1979) that depict Chicago Cubs baseball legends Ernie Banks (born 1931) and Fergie Jenkins (born 1943).

The station architecture here is functional and fairly non decorative, but the murals inside the waiting area after the turnstiles are a nice touch. Created by Steve Musgrave, they depict several Chicago Cubs' favourites, including Ryan Sandberg and Billy Williams. The murals are rendered in a muscular type of realism, and if you put your ear close to one of them, you might just hear the crack of the ball leaving the bat. That sound could also be coming from Wrigley Field, which is the next stop on the tour.

2
From the station, turn right and walk west on West Addison Street. After crossing over North Sheffield Avenue, stand in front of the large statue at the northwest corner of West Addison Street and North Sheffield Avenue.

Wrigley Field has been home to the Chicago Cubs baseball team since 1916. It has also been the scene of many disappointments, as the Cubs have not made it to a World Series since 1945. The stadium is known as the 'Friendly Confines', and perhaps its best-known feature is the ivy that grows along the wall in the outfield. The park has a great atmosphere in which to see a baseball game, though procuring tickets can be difficult. The park is also the inspiration for the surrounding neighbourhood's nickname, 'Wrigleyville'. The statue in front depicts the well-known Cubs announcer Harry Caray, who remains a beloved icon for many fans, despite having passed away in 1998.

3
Continue walking west alongside Wrigley Field on West Addison Street for one block to the northeast corner of West Addison Street and North Clark Street. Take a peek at the iconic red and white sign of Wrigley Field and then turn left to walk south on Clark Street for about 10 paces.

Located at 3541 North Clark Street, the iO Theater is part of the comedy fabric of Chicago that includes such venues as Second City and the Annoyance Theater. This improvisational comedy venue has produced a number of comedic

DISTANCE **2 miles (3.2km)**

ALLOW **2.5 hours**

START **CTA train station on West Addison Street**

FINISH **CTA bus stop on North Lake Shore Drive**

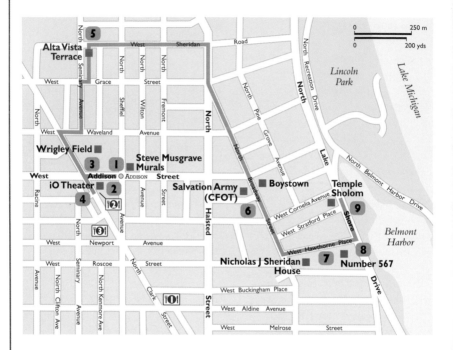

luminaries, including Chris Farley (1964–97), Tim Meadows (born 1961) and the late, great Del Close (1934–99), inventor of the long form improvisation known as the *Harold*. Shows here are inexpensive and there are a few late-night offerings that are entirely free.

IO THEATER;

http://chicago.ioimprov.com

4 Turn around and walk north on Clark Street for one block to its intersection with West Waveland Avenue. Turn right onto West Waveland Avenue and walk one block east to its intersection with North Seminary Avenue. Turn left onto North Seminary Avenue and walk one block north to its intersection with North Alta Vista Terrace. Then proceed north to join North Alta Vista Terrace.

In the late 1890s, terraced (row) houses were all the rage in Chicago and Samuel Eberly Gross (1843–1913) was a developer who kept in touch with the pulse of

residential preferences. This charming set of terraced (row) houses, known as Alta Vista Terrace was constructed in 1904. With some exceptions, all of the buildings are made of Roman brick and this elegant street offers a welcome respite from the sometime riotous atmosphere surrounding Wrigley Field.

5 Continue walking north on Alta Vista Terrace to its intersection with West Sheridan Road. Turn right onto West Sheridan Road and walk five blocks east to its intersection with North Broadway Street (note along the way Bryon Street turns into West Sheridan Road). Turn right onto North Halsted Street and walk south for one block, and then turn left onto North Broadway Street. Continue walking south for two blocks until you reach the intersection of West Addison Street and North Broadway Street.

This part of Lakeview is known as 'Boystown', as it is the epicentre of Chicago's GLBT community. The area has had a sizeable gay, lesbian, bisexual and

ABOVE: AN AERIAL VIEW OF THE GOLD COAST

transgender population for three decades, and the community sponsors a large Gay Pride parade every summer. An interesting local landmark is the Tudor Revival mansion in manicured grounds on the corner that serves as the Salvation Army College for Officers' Training.

6 Continue walking south on North Broadway Street for three blocks until reaching its intersection with West Hawthorne Place. Turn left onto West Hawthorne Place and stay on the south side of the street. Walk five paces to 587 West Hawthorne Place.

This stretch of West Hawthorne Place represents a mere fragment of what was once a substantial area of grand single-family homes scattered close to Lake Michigan. The Nicholas J. Sheridan House is an excellent example of the Craftsman style, and it features decorative glass and a prominent balcony roof.

7 Walk 10 more paces east on West Hawthorne Place to the house at 567 West Hawthorne Place.

Herman Hettler was a lumber merchant of some means, and his former Queen Anne home is distinguished by its expansive round bay and turret.

8 Walk east on West Hawthorne Place to the intersection with North Lake Shore Drive. Turn left and walk north on Lake Shore Drive (the interior street, not the six-line road across the divider) one block to the

WHERE TO EAT

[IOI] ANDALOUS,
3307 North Clark Street;
Tel: 773-281-6885.
Nice Moroccan spot featuring couscous and excellent *pastille* (layered chicken pie with almonds and herbs). $$

[IOI] SALT AND PEPPER DINER,
3537 North Clark Street;
Tel: 773-883-9800.
A lively jukebox, cheap pitchers of beer and a varied menu at this traditional American diner. $

[IOI] UBERSTEIN,
3748 North Clark Street;
Tel: 773-883-0300.
Friendly bar serving Hofbrau in German-style steins (earthenware mugs), plus pretzels and bratwurst. $

northwest corner of West Stratford Place and North Lake Shore Drive.

Temple Sholom was built in the Byzantine fashion in 1930, and the stylized elements include elaborate column capitals, friezes and stained glass windows. The entire project was conceived by architects Loebl, Schlossman and Demuth while they were still in graduate school.

9 Walk north alongside the temple to the CTA bus stop that is directly in front of the building.

Transit Architecture in the Loop

View grand architectural statements and smaller gems, samples of the city's compelling buildings constructed to serve the railroad industry.

Starting at the Santa Fe building is a great way to get a sense of the commanding structures that were built to support the various endeavours of the railroad industry in and around Chicago. It was constructed as the Railway Exchange in 1904 and for much of the first half of the 20th century the building was dominated by the hustle and bustle of the profitable freight and passenger head offices of various railroad companies. Chicago's elevated train system was completed in 1897 and, as it went in a circle around the central business district, it was nicknamed 'the Loop'. Visiting the Quincy Street station is a bit of a trip down transit memory lane, as it offers a glimpse into what a Loop station from the 1890s looked like. The tour also stops by the two remaining large passenger rail stations: Union Station was built during the last hurrah of old-school passenger stations, and it has the gravitas-filled waiting room to prove it, while the Ogilvie Transportation Center is a new take on the modern train station.

After exiting the CTA station, walk east on East Adams Street for one block to its intersection with South Michigan Avenue. Turn south onto Michigan Avenue and walk south one more block to the northwest corner of West Jackson Boulevard and South Michigan Avenue.

Distinguished by a gleaming terracotta façade and a top floor that features large porthole windows, the building standing here, finished in 1904, was home to a railway exchange. Many railroads had their Chicago offices in the building, and it is still topped by the distinctive 'Santa Fe' sign. While the railroads have since left the structure, you should definitely walk in to look over the Chicago Architecture Foundation's free exhibits and gift shop.

2 Cross over South Michigan Avenue to the east side of the street and walk 20 paces or so to the Van Buren entrance to the Metra Electric South Shore Line.

Chicago has been borrowing design and planning ideas from the French capital, Paris, for the past decade. Some of the best-known trans-Atlantic additions are the large planters that have been placed in the middle of many boulevards in the city. Here is a much more obvious icon of Paris, the famous Art Nouveau entrance used by the Paris Métro system. Originally designed by Hector Guimard (1867–1942), this cast-iron and limestone entryway was installed here in Chicago in 2002.

WHERE TO EAT

⌷O⌷ LOU MITCHELL'S RESTAURANT,
565 West Jackson Boulevard;
Tel: 312-939-3111.
At the start of the fabled Route 66, Lou Mitchell's has been serving up breakfast for over 80 years. $$$

⌷②⌷ CAL'S LIQUORS,
400 South Wells Street;
Tel: 312-922-6392.
Cal's is a favourite drink haunt for bike messengers and other denizens of the South Loop. $$$

⌷③⌷ PLYMOUTH RESTAURANT AND BAR,
327 South Plymouth Court;
Tel: 312-362-1212.
All-day breakfast, mini-burgers and a rooftop garden are reasons to stop off at the Plymouth. $$$

3 Walk about 10 paces south along South Michigan Avenue to the prominent statues depicting a pair of Native Americans.

Cast by sculptor Ivan Mestrovic (1883–1962) in 1928, these two 17ft (5m) high bronze figures depict two Native Americans. One is hurling a spear and the other is releasing an arrow. You will immediately notice that the weapons aren't actually depicted, so you will have to close your eyes and imagine these two figures hurling their projectiles down

113

DISTANCE **2.75 miles (4.4km)**

ALLOW **2.5 hours**

START **CTA train station on East Adams Street**

FINISH **CTA train station at West Lake Street and North Jefferson Street**

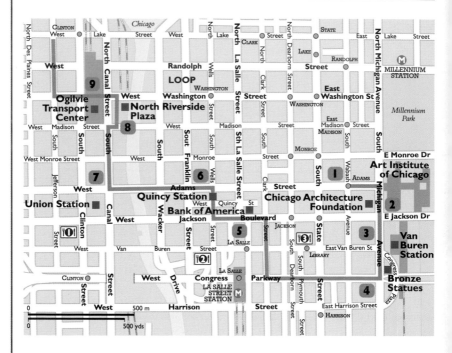

Congress Parkway towards the rush of commuters braving the local traffic jam.

4 Cross west over South Michigan Avenue to walk west along East Congress Parkway. Be careful, as this is a very busy street. Continue walking west along East Congress Parkway for four blocks to its intersection with South Clark Street. Turn right onto South Clark Street and walk two blocks north to West Jackson Boulevard. At West Jackson Boulevard, turn left and walk

along the north side of West Jackson Boulevard. Near the northeast corner of West Jackson Boulevard and South La Salle Street, you will see a small bronze plaque at eye level on the Bank of America building.

The Bank of America building (formerly the Illinois Merchants Bank Building) isn't a bad pile of bricks, but the main attraction here is the bronze plaque erected in 1971 by the Midwest Railway Historical Society. On this site in 1883,

the major railroad companies of the United States met to adopt the standard time system. It's rather mind-boggling to consider the sheer power of these companies in the 19th century—this transformation (which took effect on 19 November 1883) standardized the time system from coast to coast.

5 Walk west along West Jackson Boulevard for one block. Turn right onto South Wells Street and walk 10 paces north to the CTA's elevated train station at the intersection of South Wells Street and West Quincy Street.

If you would like to see what a traditional elevated station looked like in the 1890s, Quincy Station is perhaps the finest restoration of the entire CTA system. Originally built in 1897, the interior of the station still has its pressed tin walls and grooved wood panelling. The renovation took three years to complete, and in 1988 the station reopened to the general public for use. You'll have to pay to enter and see some of the period advertisements on the platform (including one for a hoop dress), but it's worth it.

6 After leaving Quincy Station, walk 10 paces north on South Wells Street to the intersection of Wells Street and West Adams Street. Turn left onto West Adams Street and walk three blocks west (crossing over the Chicago River) to Union Station at the southwest corner of South Canal Street and West Adams Street.

In the golden age of American railroad travel, Chicago's Union Station was a place where celebrities and the hoi polloi would switch trains while travelling from the East Coast to the West Coast, or vice versa. They might step off the train and spend a night in the luxury of the Drake Hotel or the Ambassador East in Chicago's Gold Coast. Today, this massive neoclassical building continues to serve as a major hub of passenger activity, as it handles both commuter trains to the suburbs and long-distance trains operated by Amtrak, the national rail company of the US. The building is usually open, so step inside through the Adams Street entrance to see the grand waiting room and look at the steps where the fateful baby carriage scene was filmed for the 1987 movie *The Untouchables* with Sean Connery and Kevin Costner.

7 When you come out of Union Station, walk north on South Canal Street for two blocks to its intersection with West Madison Street. Turn right and walk about 10 paces. Just before crossing the Chicago River, turn left into the plaza area in front of 2 North Riverside Plaza.

This is truly the right place to yell out 'Stop the presses'. There aren't actually any presses here now, but Riverside Plaza was the home of the *Chicago Daily News* from 1929 to 1979. The paper folded for good in 1979, and a piece of newspaper history was gone forever. This art deco building has some notable depictions of the history of printing engraved into the

first floor along the plaza. It's also a rather remarkable public space, and one would hope that future developments along the Chicago River take their cue from this smartly planned plaza.

8 Continue walking north through the plaza to West Washington Street. At West Washington Street, take a left and walk west one block to the Ogilvie Transportation Center.

In many ways, the Ogilvie Transportation Center represents the contemporary state of railroad station architecture in the United States. Named after a long-time supporter of passenger rail, Richard B. Ogilvie (1923–88), the shiny glass and steel head-house of this station also includes an adjacent 42-storey financial services building. The building and station were completed in 1987, and trains leave for the northern and western suburbs of Chicago from the Ogilvie Transportation Center.

9 Either jump on a commuter train for the suburb of your choice here, or walk back outside to West Washington Street and continue west on Washington Street for about 20 paces to North Jefferson Street. At North Jefferson Street, turn right and walk north two blocks to the CTA train station at North Jefferson Street and West Lake Street.

ABOVE: COMMUTER TRAINS DEPARTING FROM BUSY UNION STATION

THE GRAND WAITING ROOM AT UNION STATION

Near South Side: Planned Communities

Along the way this walk takes in everything from modernist architecture to the humble planned subdivision of the Groveland Park.

The walk starts at the Illinois Institute of Technology (IIT) campus—go during the day as there are opportunities to look inside some buildings—which is dominated by the influence of modernist architect and planner Mies van der Rohe (1886–1969). Moving on, you enter the area known as Bronzeville, which was the heart of Chicago's African-American community for decades. As middle-class people left in the 1960s and 1970s, the neighbourhood fell into a steep decline, though gentrification of the area started in the late 1990s. Fragments of this storied past can be seen in a variety of buildings. Close to Lake Michigan, you get a chance to see another type of planned community in the quaint layout of Groveland Park. The 19th-century cottages along the north side of the park have been demolished, but the south side still offers a slice of this planned community originally developed by US Senator Stephen Douglas (1813–61), known as the 'Little Giant' due to his diminutive stature.

1 After leaving the CTA train station at 35th Street, turn right and walk 10 paces to the intersection of East 35th Street and South State Street. Cross over to the west side of South State Street, turn right and walk 20 paces north to the S. R. Crown Hall on the Illinois Institute of Technology (IIT) campus, which will be on your left.

Unswerving in his devotion to modernism, Ludwig Mies van der Rohe emmigrated from Germany to the US in 1938 to become a professor at the Armour Institute of Technology, which then became the Illinois Institute of Technology. He established a plan of graceful symmetry for the growing campus, and the S. R. Crown Hall, completed in 1956, remains one of his greatest works. With its welded steel frames painted black and its open space plan, it provides the flexibility to create effective spaces for the study of architecture.

2 Back on South State Street, turn left to walk 20 paces to the intersection of 33rd Street and South State Street. Cross over to the east side of State Street and walk north to the McCormick Tribune Campus Center.

Finished in 2003, the McCormick Tribune Campus Center was the first building by noted Dutch architect Rem Koolhaas (born 1944) to be built in the US. The interior of the building is perhaps the most compelling, in no small part due to the Founders Wall in the lobby, which depicts the seven pivotal figures in the IIT's history, including Mies van der Rohe and founder Philip Danforth Armour, Sr. (1832–1901). The most notable design feature is that the CTA elevated train passes over it in a stainless steel tube designed to minimize noise flow. Regrettably, the campus centre also acquired the nickname 'Building Under The Tracks', which makes for an unfortunate acronym.

MIES VAN DE ROHE SOCIETY;
http://mies.iit.edu/tours

3 Turn around after leaving the campus centre and walk south back down South State Street to its intersection with East 33rd Street. Turn left on East 33rd Street and walk two blocks east to South Indiana Avenue. Turn right to walk south on South Indiana Avenue. Walk one block to East 34th Street and continue walking on the east side of Indiana Avenue for 10 paces until reaching 3435 South Indiana Avenue.

This modest three-storey building was built as a synagogue, but from 1920 to 1960 it served as the headquarters of the *Chicago Defender*, arguably the United States' finest African-American newspaper. Columns by Langston Hughes (1902–67) graced its pages, and passionate editorials urged African-Americans in the South to travel north for a better life.

4 Continue walking south on Indiana Avenue to its intersection with East 35th Street. Turn left onto East 35th Street and walk two blocks east to South Calumet Avenue. Turn left onto

A STEEL TUBE CARRIES THE CTA ELEVATED RAILWAY OVER THE MCCORMICK TRIBUNE CAMPUS CENTER

DISTANCE **2.75 miles (4.4km)**

ALLOW **3 hours**

START **CTA train station on East 35th Street (35th-Bronzeville-IIT)**

FINISH **CTA train station on East 35th Street (35th-Bronzeville-IIT)**

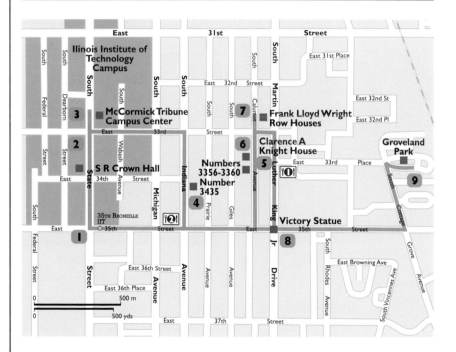

South Calumet Avenue and walk north on the west side of the street to 3356 to 3360 South Calumet Avenue.

Built around 1890, this trio of town houses has the heavy brickwork of the Richardsonian Romanesque architectural style. The best touches are on No. 3360, which has limestone carvings of dragons.

5 Walk a few paces north to the Clarence A. Knight house at 3322 South Calumet Avenue.

This house brings together oversize Romanesque corner towers and a number of Gothic details, such as the entrance. Built in 1891, it also features rusticated orange stone and Roman brick, which makes for a rather novel colour scheme.

6 Walk north to the intersection of East 33rd Street and South Calumet Avenue. Continue north across East 33rd Street and cross over to the east side of Calumet Avenue. Walk 10 paces north to the Robert W. Roloson houses at 3213–3219 South Calumet Avenue.

Frank Lloyd Wright (1869–1959) made several plans for terraced (row) houses, but this set located on Calumet Avenue was the only one executed in its entirety. Completed in 1894, the houses were built as a solid form of investment for grain merchant Robert W. Roloson. The terracotta panels have the organic and free-flowing carvings associated with architect Louis Sullivan (1856–1924).

7 Turn around on Calumet Avenue and walk back about 10 paces to the intersection with East 33rd Street. Turn left on to East 33rd Street and walk east one block to South Martin Luther King Jr. Drive. Turn right and walk south two blocks to the intersection of East 35th Street and Martin Luther King Jr. Drive.

At the intersection of East 35th Street and Martin Luther King Drive, the 1928 bronze statue entitled *Victory* was installed as a tribute to the US Army's 370th Infantry, 93rd Division, which was an African-American unit in World War I. It was appropriately placed here in the heart of Chicago's historic African-American community, and there is an annual remembrance every Memorial Day.

8 Continue walking east on East 35th Street for two blocks as far as South Cottage Grove Avenue. Turn left on to South Cottage Grove Avenue and walk north one block to East Groveland

WHERE TO EAT

🍴 MISSISSIPPI RICK'S,
3351 South Martin Luther King Drive;
Tel: 312-791-0090.
Part of the soul food belt of Chicago, Rick's specializes in rib tips, fish and chicken. $

🍴 TAURUS FLAVORS,
106 East 35th Street;
Tel: 312-842-7871.
Cheap submarine sandwiches are the main reason to visit this informal eatery. $

Park Avenue. Turn right and walk about 10 paces east along Groveland Park.

In the 1850s this area offered relief from the growing congestion in the central city and easy access via the Illinois Central Railroad. US Senator Stephen Douglas (known for his debates with Abraham Lincoln) developed Groveland Park in the 1850s as a planned subdivision. The homes on the south side of the street date from the 1880s; the gardener's lodge at 601 East Groveland Park Avenue resembles an oversized dollhouse.

9 Walk west back along Groveland Park Avenue to South Cottage Grove Avenue. Turn left and walk south one block to East 35th Street. Turn right onto East 35th Street and walk eight blocks west back to the CTA station at at the intersection of East 35th Street and South State Street.

South Loop: Boom, Bust and Back

Walking the South Loop reveals a real mix of architectural styles, from a Romanesque train station to a 20th-century tower-block jail.

The South Loop area started to boom in the late 19th century as passenger and freight trains pulled into Dearborn Station (the terminus of eight railroad companies) to unload thousands of fresh arrivals. At the same time the nearby area around South Michigan Avenue was becoming a place of conspicuous hostelry, with the Blackstone Hotel setting up near East Balbo. Back near Dearborn Station, the printing industries were flourishing and they began to construct numerous buildings to serve their needs. Moving north through the South Loop, the area became a place for signature architects to add their stamp on the early days of the skyscraper. Structures like the Monadnock and the Manhattan Building remain popular sights for those interested in the evolution of tower–block buildings. A visit to the Metropolitan Correctional Center offers a novel approach to housing prisoners, while the Auditorium Building on South Michigan Avenue is Dankmar Adler and Louis Sullivan's finest work.

1 After leaving the CTA bus stop, walk across to the northwest corner of East Balbo Drive and South Michigan Avenue, to the Blackstone Hotel.

Chicago was once full of political malfeasance, and political party bosses used to meet in hotel rooms to broker deals. The grand Blackstone Hotel was the place that gave rise to the expression 'smoke-filled room', and it was also known as the 'Hotel of Presidents' in the 20th century, as many US presidents spent a night or two here. The Blackstone's distinguishing features include its pitched mansard roof (characteristic of the Second Empire style) and the terracotta detailing around the windows.

2 Walk north about five paces on South Michigan Avenue to the Spertus Institute of Jewish Studies.

Opened in 2007, the new home of the Spertus Institute of Jewish Studies represents a dramatic and welcome change along Michigan Avenue. Designed by the firm of Krueck & Sexton, the building's façade is entirely made of glass, intended to symbolize the transparency and public nature of the institute. The folds in the glass relate and interact with the projecting bay windows of nearby buildings along Michigan Avenue.
SPERTUS INSTITUTE OF JEWISH STUDIES;
www.spertus.edu

3 Turn around and walk five paces south on South Michigan Avenue to

WHERE TO EAT

|O| EDWARDO'S NATURAL PIZZA RESTAURANT,
521 South Dearborn Street;
Tel: 312-939-3366.
Classic Chicago deep-dish pizza here, along with a selection of salads and a thin-crust option as well. $

|O| YOLK,
1120 South Michigan Avenue;
Tel: 312-789-9655.
A breakfast spot only open until the early afternoon, where they do a mean banana-nut French toast and other such items. $$$

|O| VILLAINS BAR & GRILL,
649 South Clark Street;
Tel: 312-565-9992.
With funky decor (including Andy Warhol prints), this recent arrival to the South Loop is a hip hangout. $$$

its intersection with East Balbo Drive. Turn right onto East Balbo Drive and walk two blocks west to South State Street. At South State Street, turn left and walk one block south to West Polk Street. Turn right onto West Polk Street and walk 10 paces to Dearborn Station.

A train station even without any trains (or tracks) remains a train station, and Dearborn Station happens to be the oldest one in the city. It was built in 1885, and its most notable feature is its Italian brick tower. The station was a

DISTANCE 2.2 miles (3.4km)

ALLOW 2.5 hours

START CTA bus stop at East Balbo Drive and South Michigan Avenue

FINISH CTA bus stop at East Congress Parkway and South Michigan Avenue

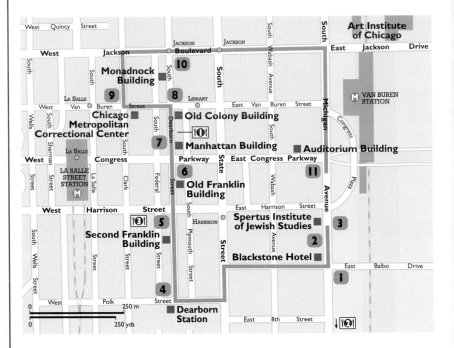

conduit for the paper supplies used in the nearby printing press buildings, and today the building houses a small retail galleria and offices.

4 Walk five paces north along the west side of South Dearborn Street to the Second Franklin Building at 720 South Dearborn Street.

From the 1880s to the 1950s this area of the South Loop was distinguished by its dense concentration of buildings dedicated to the various printing trades. Now converted to apartments, above the main entrance to the Second Franklin Building you will see tilework by Oskar Gross (1871–1963) depicting the history of the printing trade.

5 Continue north on South Dearborn Street to its intersection with West Harrison Street. Cross to the east side of South Dearborn Street and walk north to the Old Franklin Building at 525 South Dearborn Street.

When you look up at this building, the first question that comes to mind is 'How does one create a massive building that allows for plenty of natural light in 1887?' The Old Franklin Building provides the perfect answer to that question with its grouped windows that use iron spandrels between brick piers. This effectively maximized the available light so that the printers could focus on their work.

6 Continue walking north along South Dearborn Street until you reach the intersection with West Congress Parkway. Walk north across Congress Parkway to the northeast corner of South Dearborn Street and Congress Parkway.

The Manhattan Building was the first tall building with an elaborate wind-bracing system, the first 16-storey building in the US, and, for a brief time, the tallest building in the world. Finished in 1891 and designed by William Le Baron Jenney (1832–1907), it features a flurry of projecting bay windows.

7 Continue walking north on South Dearborn Street for about 10 paces to the southeast corner of South Dearborn Street where it joins West Van Buren Street.

It's hard to miss the Old Colony Building as its lovely corner bays round out this early skyscraper nicely. The Old Colony was also the first building in the US to use the decorative portal arches to brace

the building against the stiff winds that find their way into the South Loop.

8 Turn left onto West Van Buren Street and walk west two blocks to the intersection with North Clark Street. Turn to the south and face the Chicago Metropolitan Correctional Center.

Described as looking like a cheese grater or a good old-fashioned IBM punch card, this decidedly non-19th-century building is in fact a prison for federal inmates. Designed by Harry Weese (1915–98) in the brutalist style (think simple concrete and no architectural ornamentation), the jail opened for business in 1975. The first nine floors contain administrative offices, the 10th floor mechanical equipment and the remaining floors contain guest rooms for those who have broken various written laws of polite society.

9 Turn around and walk north on North Clark Street for one block to the intersection with West Jackson Boulevard. Turn right and walk east another block to the southeast corner of Jackson Boulevard and South Federal Street.

Named after a prominent mountain in New Hampshire, the Monadnock Building is one of the tallest masonry load-bearing buildings in the world. The northern half of the building has walls that are 6ft (1.8m) thick and when it was completed in 1891 the building began to sink into the ground due to its weight. In constructional counterpoise, the southern half of this tremendous building utilized steel frame construction.

10 Walk four blocks east on West Jackson Boulevard to the intersection with South Michigan Avenue. Turn right onto South Michigan Avenue and walk south two blocks to the northwest corner of South Michigan Avenue and East Congress Parkway.

The Auditorium Building could also be called 'When Adler Met Sullivan', as it represents a merging of the work of two architectural giants of the 19th century. Dankmar Adler (1844–1900) was renowned for his acoustical and engineering mettle and Louis Sullivan (1856–1924) was changing the direction of American architectural through his belief that 'form follows function', which would lead the way to modernism in subsequent decades. Finished in 1889, the Auditorium Building was designed to serve as a home for a variety of cultural institutions, including an opera company. It was truly a mixed-use building, as it also contained a 400-room hotel and rental offices. From the Michigan Avenue side, you will notice the substantial base of rusticated granite rising up to a smooth vertical layer of Bedford limestone. Step inside the lobby and walk up the grand staircase to the second floor lobby to spend a few moments watching the lively street life along Michigan Avenue.

11 Cross east over South Michigan Avenue to the CTA bus stop.

THE AUDITORIUM BUILDING BY DANKMAR ADLER AND LOUIS SULLIVAN

THE VAST AUDITORIUM BUILDING THEATER—ITS PERFECT ACOUSTICS ARE WORLD RENOWNED

The Mansions of Lincoln Park

On this walk you will see some of the grand houses that characterized the area's initial flourish of haute architecture in the 1880s and 1890s.

Lincoln Park is known for its austere and decorative mansions in an area favoured by Chicago's families of distinction. After stepping off the CTA platform, the first stop is the McCormick Row Houses. Walking through the two parallel rows of houses surrounded by the more riotous atmosphere of the DePaul University campus, some might find it a bit odd that this is such a popular place to live. It's actually quite bucolic, and the campus isn't a bad place to wander on your own if you have a little time. A few blocks away past the hustle and bustle of a prominent six-way intersection you will come across tree-lined West Fullerton Parkway. Constantly busy with traffic going to and coming from nearby Lake Michigan, it still makes for a pleasant walk, particularly during summer and spring. Plan this tour in daylight as there are great photo opportunities. You can also go inside the Elks National Memorial Headquarters (a fraternal organization), although you can't partake in any mystical rituals.

1 Walk out of the CTA train station to West Fullerton Avenue. Turn right and walk 10 paces or so to an iron gate on the right. Pass through the gate to enter the DePaul University campus. Walk south about 10 paces and turn to the left; here you will see the McCormick Row Houses.

Sitting squarely in the middle of DePaul University's campus, this collection of Queen Anne-style terraced (row) houses provides a pleasant contrast to the prevailing architecture on campus, which is largely institutional and bland. The row houses were built between 1882 and 1889 to provide rental income from the McCormick Theological Seminary. When the seminary decamped to the South Side in 1975, there was a community fracas over whether the row houses should be preserved. Fortuitously, they got the nod to stay, and they survive as an excellent example of late 19th-century planning ingenuity.

2 Walk east through the row houses, and then turn to the left and walk north five paces or so back through another iron gate to West Fullerton Avenue. Turn right onto West Fullerton and walk five paces east to its intersection with North Lincoln Avenue and North Halsted Street (it's a busy six-way intersection, so mind your step!). Cross north over West Fullerton Parkway, and then turn and walk northeast across to the east side of North Lincoln Avenue. Walk 10 paces northwest to the Biograph Theater.

WHERE TO EAT

🍴 **HEMA'S KITCHEN II,**
2411 North Clark Street;
Tel: 773-529-1705.
The various naan are a real treat at this Indian eatery and you are welcome to bring your own wine and beer. **$**

🍴 **THE OTHER SIDE,**
2436 North Clark Street;
Tel: 773-525-8238.
At first glance a typical bar, but there's more when you consider the generous drink specials and nightly food specials, including pizza and tater tots. **$**

🍴 **CREPE & COFFEE PALACE,**
2433 North Clark Street;
Tel: 773-404-1300.
Mint tea, Turkish coffee and sweet and savoury crêpes are a feature of this pleasant stop for lunch. **$**

Now home to the Victory Gardens theatre group, this site is best known as the place where Public Enemy Number 1 John Dillinger (1903–34) met his end in the alley south of the building. Dillinger was a violent gun-toting criminal whose forte was robbing banks and engaging in other socially irresponsible acts during the Great Depression. The famous Lady in Red (who was actually wearing an orange skirt) tipped off federal investigators that he was taking in a movie at the Biograph on 22 July 1934.

DISTANCE **1.75 miles (2.8km)**

ALLOW **2 hours**

START **CTA train station on West Fullerton Avenue**

FINISH **CTA bus stop at West Diversey Parkway and North Sheridan Road**

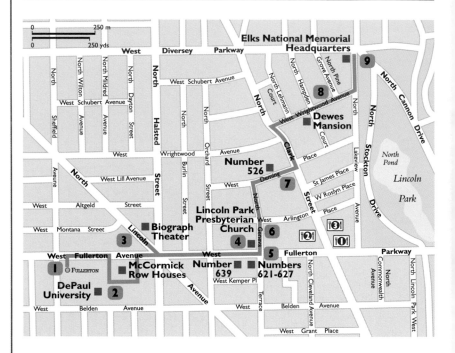

They shot him as he left the theatre, and that was the end of Dillinger.

3 Walk roughly 10 paces back down North Lincoln Avenue to the intersection with North Halsted Street and West Fullerton Avenue. Turn left and cross over to the east side of North Halsted Street. Then cross south over West Fullerton Avenue (which becomes a parkway, but remains the same street) and turn left and walk one block east on Fullerton Parkway to North Orchard Street. Cross east over North Orchard Street and continue walking east to 639 West Fullerton Parkway.

You are looking at a fairly standard grand mansion for this tree-lined stretch of Lincoln Park, but wait a minute—are those carved dog profiles above the entrance to the house? Or are they perhaps people with unusually pointy noses? Get a bit closer and decide for yourself; it's an unusual, playful feature that is sure to amuse.

4 Continue walking for about five paces along West Fullerton Parkway to the houses that span from 621 to 627 West Fullerton Parkway.

These stoic houses from the late 1880s are distinguished by their massive wooden porches, which look just about right for sitting out and drinking lemonade with friends and family. Their best features, however, are the discs that adorn the cornice of the porches like so many errant UFOs.

5 Walk five paces east to the intersection of West Fullerton Parkway and North Geneva Terrace. Cross north over Fullerton Parkway to the northwest corner of Fullerton and North Geneva Terrace. Do so carefully, as the stop signs are treated as suggestions along this stretch of road.

Built in the early days of Lincoln Park's social dominance among residential neighbourhoods, Lincoln Park Presbyterian Church was finished in

ABOVE: OUTSIDE THE ELKS NATIONAL MEMORIAL HEADQUARTERS

1888 and an addition was added in 1898. The corners of the building are gently rounded and the weightiness is achieved by stacking discs of sandstone to create ponderous vertical elements. The church has been steeple-less since 1970.

6 Walk north along North Geneva Terrace for one block until reaching the intersection with West Deming Place. Cross over to the north side of Deming Place, turn right and walk five paces to 526 West Deming Place.

As arguably the grandest mansion of this stretch of very nice mansions, the William C. Groetzinger house (finished in 1895) displays such Gothic features as pointed arches and a large porch complete with stone columns for a touch of permanence. It's exactly the type of domicile that would have attracted the upper-crust businessman and his family to this area in the 1890s.

7 Continue east along West Deming Place for five paces until reaching the intersection with North Clark Street. Cross over to the east side of North Clark Street and turn left to walk north on Clark, and then one block north to West Wrightwood Avenue. Turn right onto West Wrightwood Avenue and walk two blocks to the southwest corner of West Wrightwood Avenue and North Hampden Court.

Built in 1896 by Adolph Cudell (1850–1910) and Arthur Hercz for the brewer Francis J. Dewes, this elaborate mansion brings together a cornucopia of architectural styles, including elements of the rococo, baroque and the Classical. There's a veritable explosion of statues clinging to the columns along the home's primary entrance on West Wrightwood, and along the top of the building you will notice a mansard roof and some nice porthole windows.

8 Continue walking east along West Wrightwood Avenue for two blocks to the intersection with North Lakeview Avenue. Turn left onto North Lakeview Avenue and walk north 15 paces to the Elks National Memorial Headquarters building.

While membership in fraternal organizations in the US has declined over the past few decades, this monument to members of the Elks who were killed in World War I stands as testimony to their numbers and influence in the early 20th century. Constructed between 1923 and 1926, the building was based on the Pantheon in Rome, and the Memorial Rotunda inside contains a wild assortment of coloured marbles and murals depicting such notions as justice, fidelity and charity.

ELKS NATIONAL MEMORIAL HEADQUARTERS;
www.elks.org/memorial

9 Walk north on North Lakeview Avenue across West Diversey Parkway to the CTA bus stop at the northwest corner of West Diversey Parkway and North Sheridan Road.

VIEW ACROSS LINCOLN PARK LAGOON OF DOWNTOWN CHICAGO

Milwaukee Avenue:
Havana to Krakow

**North Milwaukee Avenue and the nearby streets have served as an
incubator for new arrivals to the city for over 120 years.**

This walk starts off from the CTA station on North California Avenue and the
first few points of interest afford a glimpse into the historic core of an area that
was once called Little Norway. The golden era of Norwegian immigration to
Chicago was in the early 1900s, and at one point the city had the third-largest
Norwegian population in the world, after the cities of Oslo and Bergen.
Winding around Logan Square and on to North Milwaukee Avenue, it's
easy to see the dominance of Latin American–themed shops north of West
Fullerton Avenue. After European immigrants like the Norwegians and others
began to leave, Puerto Ricans, Cubans and Mexicans came to set up *taquerias*,
sandwich stores and clothing shops here. Marching up Milwaukee Avenue, in
the blocks before Belmont Avenue, is a bit like approaching the outskirts of
Warsaw. It's not hard to see why the area is known as Polish Village,
and specialty stores selling everything from Polish airfares to meat-based
soups are cheek by jowl along the street.

After leaving the very historic CTA station at North California Avenue, continue a few paces north on North California Avenue to the intersection with West Lyndale Street. Turn left onto West Lyndale Street and continue west for four blocks to the intersection with North Kedzie Avenue. Cross over to the west side of this major thoroughfare, taking great care, and walk about five paces north to West Belden Avenue. Cross north over West Belden Avenue and walk 10 paces to the Chicago Norske Club, which is located at 2350 North Kedzie Avenue.

In the 1870s and 1880s, Norwegian immigrants to Chicago moved further north and west to this part of Logan Square. Upon their arrival they began to set up a range of social and cultural institutions, including several churches and this decorative social club building. The Chicago Norske Club takes its cue from traditional Norwegian vernacular forms and the heavy brackets and curious dragons are some of the more noticeable features utilized on this small structure.

2 Continue walking north on North Kedzie Boulevard for three blocks until you reach the Norwegian Lutheran Memorial Church, which is located at 2614 North Kedzie Avenue.

This Norwegian Lutheran Memorial Church was one of the pre-eminent Norwegian institutions in the area, which a century ago was known as Little Norway. Completed in 1905, the church

WHERE TO EAT

🍴 LULA CAFÉ,
2537 North Kedzie Avenue;
Tel: 773-489-9554.
Artisanal and organic choices abound, and recent offerings have included peanut satay noodles and a shitake mushroom *quesadilla*. $$

🍴 RED APPLE BUFFET,
3121 North Milwaukee Avenue;
Tel: 773-588-5781.
Pierogis (Polish dumplings), sausage, cabbage-themed products and lots of meat are offered at this very cheap Polish buffet restaurant. $

🍴 CAFETERIA MARIANAO,
2246 North Milwaukee Avenue;
Tel: 773-278-4533.
Basic Cuban sandwich shop that serves the standard roasted pork, ham, cheese and pickles combination. $

still holds services in Norwegian for descendants of the original immigrants.

3 Cross northwest over West Logan Boulevard to the Illinois Centennial Monument, which stands in the middle of Logan Square.

This square (which is more oval than square in shape) sits at the northwest corner of the Chicago Parks Boulevard System, which was designed by landscape architect Jens Jensen (1860–1951) and

DISTANCE **2.5 miles (4km)**

ALLOW **2.5 hours**

START **CTA train station on North California Avenue**

FINISH **CTA bus stop on North Milwaukee Avenue**

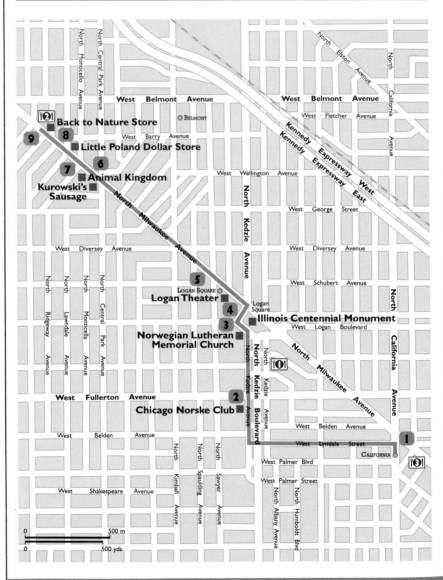

OPPOSITE: NORWEGIAN LUTHERAN MEMORIAL CHURCH

architect Daniel Burnham (1846–1912). Within the oval you will notice the 68ft (21m) tall Doric column designed by Henry Bacon (1866–1924) to celebrate the centennial anniversary of Illinois' admission to statehood. The column was finished in 1918, and you can get up close and peer into the faces of the farmers and Native Americans that grace the base of this monument.

4 Cross north and continue out of the square to North Milwaukee Avenue. Be careful crossing here as it is a rather confusing intersection and is always very busy with traffic. Stay on the west side of North Milwaukee Avenue and walk north for about 10 paces to the Logan Theater.

Tucked in among mobile phone stores, taco joints and low-cost haberdasheries is the Logan Theatre. It has a grand covered entrance but the real deal here is the very cheap second (or third) run movies. It's a bit worn-down, but stick around for a show and some popcorn as a way to pass the time.

5 Walk five blocks north on the west side of North Milwaukee Avenue. After you pass North Central Park Avenue, walk another 10 paces north on Milwaukee Avenue until you reach Kurowski's Sausage shop

Even if you are a vegan, the shifting meat theatre that is Kurowski's Sausage may still be intriguing. The main show here

ABOVE: POLISH SAUSAGES AT A MARKET, POLISH VILLAGE; OPPOSITE: A PET STORE, NORTH MILWAUKEE AVENUE

is the interaction between customers ordering meat and the butchers, but there is also an astonishing range of Polish candies, baked goods, teas and other items suitable for a picnic.

6 After leaving the sausage shop, turn left and walk north on Milwaukee Avenue to the next storefront, which contains the Animal Kingdom.

'Kingdom' is a bit of an overstatement, but this rather bizarre pet store/ menagerie should not be missed. Walk in to the display area in the back to see a wide range of traditional pets (beagles, long-haired cats, etc.) and a host of oddities, including a toucan and a few other non-pet store type of creatures.

7 Continue walking north to the intersection with North Lawndale Avenue. At Lawndale Avenue, cross over to the east side of North Milwaukee Avenue and walk north to the Little Poland Dollar Store.

This store offers an explosion of low-cost Polish themed goods (most of which are probably from China), including football jerseys, Pope John Paul II icons, flags and a number of items whose ultimate purpose is hard to discern. Again, it's well worth a stop, and it's hard to miss as it generally has loud Polish rock music blasting from its entrance.

8 Continue walking north on North Milwaukee Avenue for another 10 paces or so until you come to the Back to Nature Store at 3101 North Milwaukee Avenue.

Run by a very pleasant Polish woman, this store carries naturopathic healing products, including balms, herbs, teas and other items that may ease jet lag and improve your general state of well-being.

9 The CTA bus stop is on the other side of North Milwaukee Avenue, so just cross over to the west side of the street to catch a bus.

Edgewater and Andersonville

Take a jaunt past a prominent pink apartment and an English-style manor house, before arriving at the cultural melting pot that is Andersonville.

The appeal of Edgewater goes back over 120 years, when families were eager to move far away from the soot-belching industry that was spreading out from the city centre. The walk starts off along the dense apartment and commercial lined street of West Bryn Mawr Avenue and takes in the Edgewater Beach Apartments building. Once upon a time, the building was part of a sprawling complex of luxurious living, but it now stands alone, decked out in pink paint. As you pass under Lake Shore Drive, you will get a look at the mosaic *Living 2007*. Returning into the heart of Edgewater, this area was covered in celery farms in the 1880s, around the time that the community we see today began to be developed. Today, this part maintains its pastoral feel, and is dominated by large houses built between the 1880s and the 1910s. Continuing west you come to Andersonville, a community that includes everything from established Swedish restaurants to gay-friendly bars and businesses and is one of Chicago's most tolerant and open-minded neighbourhoods.

After leaving the CTA train station, walk east along West Bryn Mawr Avenue for one block to the northeast corner of Bryn Mawr Avenue and North Winthrop Avenue.

This stretch of West Bryn Mawr Avenue in Edgewater contains a number of overlooked architectural gems, and the Belle Shore Apartment Hotel is the first highlight you come to. Finished right before the onset of the Great Depression in 1929, the terracotta façade contains a number of stunning pieces of ornamentation, including an Egyptian frieze and the stylized 'Y' device, which represents the branches of the Chicago River and which also happens to be one of the city's unofficial logos. The building was remodelled several years ago, and it now contains more than 100 modest kitchenette apartments.

2 Cross over to the south side of Bryn Mawr Avenue and continue walking east along Bryn Mawr Avenue to the southeast corner of North Kenmore Avenue and West Bryn Mawr Avenue.

Perched at the corner of Bryn Mawr Avenue and Kenmore since 1908, this Tudor Revival apartment building was built by British-born architect John Edmund Oldaker Pridmore (1864–1940). Pridmore was a resident of Edgewater for many years, and he went all out with this august building. Originally it had only six apartments, each with 12 to 16 rooms, and two of the apartments had ballrooms. He left a touch of the UK in the form of

the royal coat of arms that hangs in the rear section of the courtyard.

3 Continue walking east on Bryn Mawr Avenue for about 10 paces and then cross over to the east side of North Sheridan Road and you'll be standing in front of the Edgewater Beach Apartments—hard to miss, as the building is painted bright pink.

When the Twenties roared, so did the Edgewater Beach Hotel complex. Finished in 1927, the complex included a luxury hotel (since demolished), a private beach, seaplane service to the Loop and the Edgewater Beach Apartments. The apartment building has been the site of some intrigue, as a rather obsessed baseball fan attempted to shoot and kill the professional baseball player Eddie Waitkus (1919–72) here in 1949. This unfortunate incident served as the

DISTANCE 1.9 miles (3km)

ALLOW 2 hours

START CTA train station on West Bryn Mawr Avenue

FINISH CTA bus stop on North Clark Street

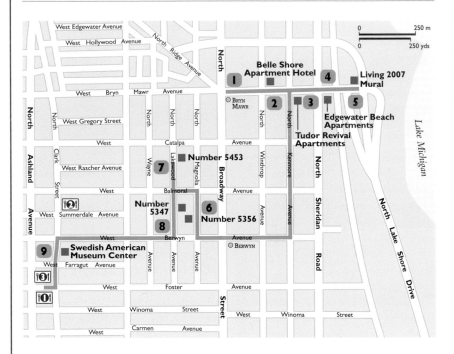

basis for Bernard Malamud's novel *The Natural*, which was later made into a movie starring Robert Redford. Take a look inside the building's lobby, paying particular attention to the wood-panelled carvings and main entrance.

4 After leaving the Edgewater Beach Apartments, cross over to the north side of Bryn Mawr Avenue and walk about 15 paces east to the large mural along the wall next to the sidewalk beneath Lake Shore Drive.

With its thousands of colourful pieces of ceramic tile, mirror and concrete, *Living 2007* is considered to be Chicago's best new piece of public art. The whole bricolage project got started when contemporary artists Tracy Van Duinen and Todd Osborne spent a year and a half talking to Edgewater residents and community groups to get a sense of the area's shared history and various experiences. After this, they gathered together a group of young people to assist with the creation and assemblage

OPPOSITE: AN AERIAL VIEW OF LAKE SHORE DRIVE AND LAKE MICHIGAN

of the work, bringing together materials to create a CTA train, a rising sun, birds rising up from the ground and dozens of other small visual vignettes.

5 Turn around to walk back west along Bryn Mawr Avenue for two blocks until you come to the intersection with North Kenmore Avenue. Turn left onto Kenmore Avenue and walk south for three blocks to West Berwyn Avenue. Turn right onto West Berwyn Avenue and continue three blocks west to North Magnolia Avenue. Turn right onto North Magnolia Avenue and walk about 20 paces north on the east side of the street to 5356 North Magnolia Avenue.

This area of Edgewater was aggressively promoted as a development away from the grime of Chicago in the 1880s and 1890s, and walking through this concentration of large houses gives an excellent idea of what the area looked like then (and now). This particular house was built by George W. Maher (1864–1926) who was a disciple of Frank Lloyd Wright (1867–1959). Finished in 1904, the building is a disarmingly simple design that includes a horizontality, which is achieved by the wide rectilinear massing.

6 Continue walking north on North Magnolia Avenue for a few paces to the intersection with West Balmoral

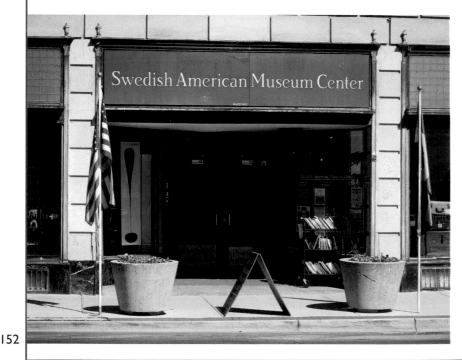

SWEDISH AMERICAN MUSEUM CENTER, A TRIBUTE TO THE SWEDISH SETTLERS OF ANDERSONVILLE

Avenue. Turn left onto West Balmoral Avenue and walk west one block to North Lakewood Avenue. Turn right onto North Lakewood Avenue and walk north 20 paces to 5453 North Lakewood Avenue.

Designed by the firm of Holabird & Roche in 1898, this house is distinguished both by its Classical-inspired second-floor bay and its overall symmetry.

7 Turn around and walk south back down North Lakewood Avenue to the intersection with West Balmoral Avenue. Cross over to the east side of North Lakewood Avenue and walk south to 5347 North Lakewood Avenue.

Amidst other fine homes along this stretch of Lakewood Avenue, this 1910 building has diamond-paned windows and a pergola-type porch that is indicative of the Craftsman style of architecture.

8 Continue walking south until you reach the intersection of West Berwyn Avenue and North Lakewood Avenue. Turn right onto Berwyn Avenue and walk a few blocks west to North Clark Street. Turn left onto North Clark Street and walk about 15 paces south to the Swedish American Museum Center.

While walking along North Clark Street you may have noticed a few Swedish-themed businesses. This section of Edgewater is known as Andersonville, and it was designated as such in the 1960s to honour the original Swedish settlers of

WHERE TO EAT

[O] HOPLEAF BAR,
5148 North Clark Street;
Tel: 773-334-9851.
Belgian Trappist ales and other upmarket beers (and food) are the focus of this neighbourhood bar in Andersonville. $$

[O] CALO RISTORANTE,
5343 North Clark Street;
Tel: 773-271-7725.
Deep-dish pizza is always a good bet here. $$

[O] SIMON'S TAVERN,
5210 North Clark Street;
Tel: 773-878-0894.
An eclectic jukebox and cheap drinks are the calling cards of this bar. $

the district. The Swedish American Museum Center has been at this site since 1987, and it includes art galleries, a Children's Museum of Immigration, a Swedish-language library and, of course, a gift shop. It also sponsors a wide range of cultural activities.

SWEDISH AMERICAN MUSEUM CENTER;
www.samac.org/

9 Continue walking south for about 10 paces along North Clark Street to West Foster Avenue. Turn right and cross the intersection to the CTA bus stop, which is on the west side of North Clark Street.

Flora and Fauna of Lincoln Park

Lincoln Park boasts good picnic spots, a zoo, the splendour of Caldwell Lily Pool and the subtropical climate of Lincoln Park Conservatory.

The history of Lincoln Park is quite fascinating; its southern half was originally a city cemetery and the remainder was created out of landfill. The park covers over 1,200 acres (486ha), and shortly after it was created it was renamed Lincoln Park in 1865 to honour US President Abraham Lincoln (1809–65). The first stop on this walk happens to be at the statue of Lincoln created by sculptor Augustus Saint-Gaudens (1848–1907). Another stop includes a visit to the Lincoln Park Zoo, founded in 1868. The first gift to the zoo was two pairs of swans from New York City's own Central Park. Since then, the zoo has grown to include an expansive primate exhibit, a clutch of sea animals and a fine merry-go-round. Further on, the Lincoln Park Conservatory beckons with its glass structure and promise of orchids, ferns and palm trees. After meandering around the Lily Pool, the walk ends at the Peggy Notebaert Nature Museum, a delightful place for children who have a penchant for butterflies.

After leaving the CTA bus stop at West North Avenue and North Clark Street, turn onto West North Avenue and walk east two blocks to North Dearborn Parkway. Turn left and walk north along the pathway into Lincoln Park for five paces.

As he steps to the podium, Abraham Lincoln looks forward into the crowd gathered to hear him speak. This is the essence of this sculpture of Illinois' favourite son created in 1887 by the noted sculptor August Saint-Gaudens. Known as *The Standing Lincoln*, the bronze sculpture is 12ft (3.6m) high. Many have drawn close to it for inspiration, including Chicago-based social reformer Jane Addams (1860–1935) who walked from the city's Near West Side to Lincoln Park 'to look at and gain magnanimous counsel, if I might, from the marvelous St Gaudens statue'.

2 Immediately north of the Lincoln statue is a path that leads to North La Salle Drive. Follow this path for about 10 paces to the northwest and keep an

eye out for a mausoleum that is located behind the Chicago Historical Society.

Seemingly out of place, this mausoleum stands as testimony to the tenacity of the Couch family. Ira Couch (1806–57) was a prominent Chicago hotelier who started in the 1830s. When he passed away in 1857, his family spent a sizeable sum to build him a mausoleum of limestone shipped in from New York. At the time, there was no Lincoln Park, but rather the city cemetery stretched from North Avenue to West Armitage Avenue near the lakefront. After public health concerns were raised due to the cemetery's presence, the city began relocating graves (and their remains) from the site. The Couch family declined to have Ira's remains removed and the mausoleum is still there today. And no one really knows whether Couch (or anyone else) is actually still entombed within ....

3 Walk north from the mausoleum for about 10 paces to North La Salle Drive. At North La Salle Drive cross over to the north side of the

155

DISTANCE 1.75 miles (2.8km)

ALLOW 3 hours

START **CTA bus stop at North Clark Street and West North Avenue**

FINISH **CTA bus stop at North Clark Street and West Fullerton Parkway**

street. Here you will find North Stockton Drive. Walk north on North Stockton Drive for approximately 40 paces to the Farm-In-The-Zoo. You'll probably see the barnyard animals and the silo as you approach the compound.

A traditional Midwestern farm is the general idea here, where you can get up close and personal with chickens, cows, sheep and pigs (and occasionally piglets). The place is perfect for children, and older city dwellers, who want to get away

from it all. There are demonstrations of cow milking and butter making, and there is a general store that sells souvenirs.
FARM-IN-THE-ZOO;
www.lpzoo.org/animals/FARM/index.php

4 After leaving the Farm-In-The-Zoo, turn right and walk 15 paces east along the path that leads over South Pond. Immediately crossing over the pedestrian bridge, look for the zoo entrance on the north side of the path. Walk inside and go north.

ABOVE: SIBERIAN TIGER, ONE OF THE RESIDENTS AT LINCOLN PARK ZOO

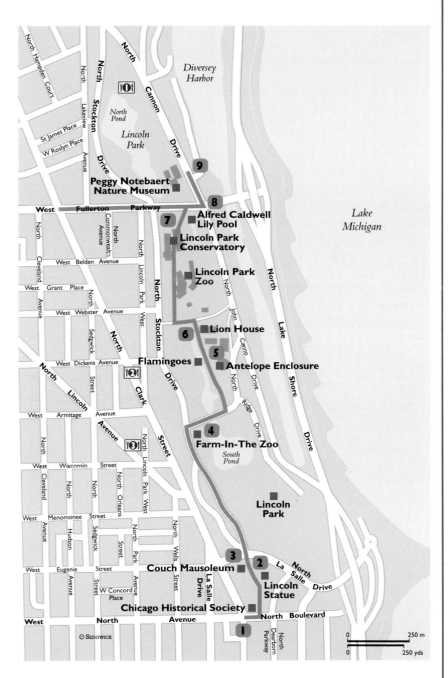

Diversey
Harbor

North
Pond

Lincoln
Park

9

**Peggy Notebaert
Nature Museum** ■

8

West   Fullerton   Parkway

7   ■ **Alfred Caldwell
Lily Pool**

■ **Lincoln Park
Conservatory**

West Belden Avenue

West Grant Place

■ **Lincoln Park
Zoo**

West Webster Avenue

6   ■ **Lion House**

5

Flamingoes ■   ■ **Antelope Enclosure**

West Dickens Avenue

West Armitage Avenue

4

Farm-In-The Zoo

South
Pond

West Wisconsin Street

■ **Lincoln
Park**

West Menomonee Street

West Eugenie Street

3   **2**

Couch Mausoleum ■   ■ **Lincoln
Statue**

W Concord
Place

Chicago Historical Society ■

1

West   North   Avenue   North Boulevard

© SEDGWICK

Lake
Michigan

0 _____ 250 m

0 _____ 250 yds

157

This part of Lincoln Park Zoo is certainly one of the largest enclosures, and it features antelope, onyx, alpaca and takin. The takin should not be missed, as it is an unusual goat antelope that is found only in the eastern Himalayas.

LINCOLN PARK ZOO;

www.lpzoo.org/

5 Continue walking north along the same path for about 30 paces. After passing the flamingoes on your left and a large food court building on the right, you will see a large brick building on the right.

While the various big cats housed in this building don't exactly look happy, this 1912 structure does offer some well-designed interior spaces for humans to admire the beautiful creatures. Along the outside of the building there are stylized lions in the brickwork, and the outside also creates pleasant naturalistic surroundings for the lions and tigers.

6 After leaving the lion house, turn to the northwest and follow the path 15 paces out of the zoo. Walk north through the formal French gardens 20 paces to the Lincoln Park Conservatory.

Open 365 days a year, the Lincoln Park Conservatory is a great place to come in from the cold or the sometimes oppressive humidity of Chicago summers. Built as part of a flourish of park improvements in the 1890s, the conservatory contains everything from orchids to ferns that have been around for millions of years, albeit not these exact ferns under the glass. During the year, the conservatory also mounts different themed flower shows.

7 After leaving the conservatory, turn right and walk to the path that runs alongside the building. Turn right onto this path and walk about 10 paces north to West Fullerton Parkway. Turn right onto West Fullerton Parkway and walk approximately 20 paces until you arrive at the entrance to the Alfred Caldwell Lily Pool.

The Caldwell Lily Pool has been through three lives since its initial construction in 1889. When it was first built, its primary function was to grow tropical water lilies. Later on, the pool was completely overhauled by the designer Alfred Caldwell (1903–98) in 1937. Caldwell made significant nods to the natural ecology of the Midwest by offering up a river that appears to have been formed by a melting glacier's flow of water. In 2001, after decades of neglect and poor maintenance, the Chicago Park District replaced invasive species with native prairie and woodland plants. The area was effectively reborn and is a fabulous place to wander around, particularly during the spring and summer when the specimens are at their best.

8 After leaving the Lily Pool, turn right onto West Fullerton Parkway and walk about 15 paces east to the intersection with North Cannon Drive. Turn left onto North Cannon Drive, and then walk north another 15 paces. Turn left again to visit the Peggy Notebaert Nature Museum.

WHERE TO EAT

🍴 NORTH POND CAFÉ,
2610 North Cannon Drive;
Tel: 773-477-5845.
Locally sourced produce and meats are used when possible at this upmarket, organic white-linen restaurant. $$$

🍴 R. J. GRUNTS,
2056 North Lincoln Park West;
Tel: 773-929-5363.
This popular burger and salad joint spawned a Chicago restaurant empire back in the early 1970s. $$

🍴 BRICK'S CHICAGO,
1909 North Lincoln Park West;
Tel: 312-255-0851.
Gourmet pizzas include the Popeye (lots of spinach and roasted garlic) and the Berzerkeley (smoked ham and artichoke hearts). $$$

The Peggy Notebaert Nature Museum was opened in 1999 and it has been a popular destination for children and families ever since. Discover the mystery of nature through the museum's exhibits, which include topics such as the Art and Science of the American Lawn, and Skyscapes: Meteorological Phenomena. Don't miss the outstanding Judy Istock Butterfly Haven, which is a 2,700sq ft (2,508sq m) greenhouse filled with over 1,000 brightly coloured butterflies.

PEGGY NOTEBAERT NATURE MUSEUM;
www.naturemuseum.org

9 After leaving the museum, walk south for about 10 paces along North Cannon Drive to West Fullerton Parkway. Turn right onto West Fullerton Parkway and walk three blocks west to the intersection with North Clark Street. Cross over to the west side of North Clark Street where you will find the CTA bus stop.

ABOVE: SKATEBOARDING IN LINCOLN PARK; OPPOSITE: LINCOLN PARK WITH A CHICAGO SKYLINE BACKDROP

From Crypts to Graves: Graceland Cemetery

On this tour you will walk among pyramids, gaze into the face of Death and learn about the last resting places of well-known Chicagoans.

Graceland was founded in 1860 by the real estate investor Thomas B. Bryan (1828–1906). Bryan knew he needed the best in the business to bring in potential occupants, so he enlisted the services of designer William Saunders. Saunders had previously worked at another cemetery in the city's North Side, so he was familiar with the intricacies of creating a site that would be tranquil. Things start off with a bit of a spooky moment as you approach the rather mysterious sculpture created by Lorado Taft (1860–1936) for the grave of hotelier Dexter Graves (1789–1844). Moving past the cemetery's chapel and mortuary crypt, you come to the Egyptian-styled tombs of lumber baron Martin Ryerson (1818–87) and brewer Peter Schoenhofen (1827–93). Making a trip around the cemetery's lake brings you to the impressive tomb of Potter (1826–1902) and Bertha Palmer (1849–1918), the dry-goods merchant and his socialite wife, and the grave marker of modernist architect Ludwig Mies van der Rohe (1886–1969).

1 After leaving the CTA bus stop at the southeast corner of North Clark Street and West Irving Park Road, walk north across West Irving Park Road. Walk into Graceland Cemetery and pause just inside the entrance gates.

To the left is the cemetery's administration building, which was built in 1896 by the design firm of Holabird & Roche. You can stop in to buy a historic map of the cemetery or just to ask any pertinent questions about the grounds.

GRACELAND CEMETERY;

www.gracelandcemetery.org

2 Turn right onto Evergreen Avenue (these are all internal roads, and bear no relationship to other streets outside the cemetery) and walk to the intersection with Glendale Avenue. Bear left and walk north five paces to the family plot of Dexter Graves, close to the intersection with Main Avenue.

Dexter Graves was an early Chicago pioneer and hotelier who rambled up to the city from Ashtabula in Ohio, in 1831. In 1909, sculptor Lorado Taft created the statue here for the plot and entitled it *Eternal Silence.*

3 Turn right onto Main Avenue and walk northwest 10 paces to the intersection with Center Avenue. Turn left onto Center Avenue and walk about 10 paces north.

No cemetery is really complete without a distinguished looking chapel and

mortuary crypt. Graceland Cemetery has both of them right here and the decision to clad them in rusticated red granite was a sound one. Along with these two buildings from 1888, a columbarium (a building for housing cremated remains) and fountain from 1996 sit side by side.

4 Walk north on Center Avenue to the next intersection. Turn right and walk northwest 10 paces to the George Pullman monument on the left.

When George Pullman (1831–97) died he was not a well-liked man in some quarters. He had called in the federal government to his company town of Pullman in 1894 to help break up striking workers, and many people would never forgive him. His grave site includes this Corinthian column and Pullman himself

163

DISTANCE **1 mile (1.6km)**

ALLOW **1.5 hours**

START **CTA bus stop at North Clark Street and West Irving Park Road**

FINISH **CTA bus stop at North Clark Street and West Irving Park Road**

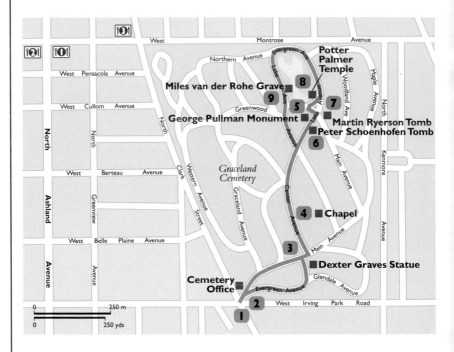

is interred underneath inside a concrete block topped with railroad ties. His family, fearing retaliation after his death, resorted to these extraordinary measures.

5 After leaving the Pullman monument walk across to the southeast side of Lake Avenue to take a look at the Peter Schoenhofen tomb.

As a Prussian in Chicago during the 1850s, it was almost assumed that Peter Schoenhofen would rise to the level of beer baron. He eventually did, and the brewing company he founded lasted over a century. His tomb resembles something out of the movie *Raiders of the Lost Ark*, a steep-sided pyramid with an Egyptian portal and a sun disc.

6 Look immediately north and you'll see an equally impressive pyramid-style tomb. Walk over to it.

Lumber baron and savvy real estate speculator Martin Ryerson was a

OPPOSITE: THE TOMB OF BEER BARON PETER SCHOENHOFEN

19th-century Chicagoan who gave away much of his fortune to the Art Institute of Chicago and the University of Chicago. Architect Louis Sullivan (1856–1924) designed his fantastic Egyptian mausoleum in 1889. Constructed out of black granite, the tomb has a respectful and eerie quality at the same time.

Potter Palmer was a dry-goods merchant who helped create the retail corridor of State Street in the city's Loop throughout the later half of the 19th century. He and his wife, a Chicagon socialite Bertha Honoré, were both laid to rest in these twin sarcophagi set in a rather fine temple of Ionic columns.

7 Turn right on Lake Avenue and walk to a path that bends west to a lake.

8 Walking north along the lake to Evergreen Avenue, turn left onto

ABOVE: THE BLACK GRANITE EGYPTIAN-STYLE TOMB OF MARTIN RYERSON

Evergreen Avenue and walk around the lake until joining Lake Avenue again. Turn left onto Lake Avenue and walk south for about 15 paces.

Mies van der Rohe set the standard for modernism's adherence to simplicity and architectural transparency and his grave marker echoes this style. Designed by his grandson, architect Dirk Lohan (born 1938), it is a simple flat slab of black

WHERE TO EAT

[O] UMAIYA CAFÉ,
1605 West Montrose Avenue;
Tel: 773-404-1109.
Sushi and Thai food at this low-key restaurant; compelling items include the winter roll, which includes white tuna, salmon and scallions. $

[O] LA SIERRA,
1637 West Montrose Avenue;
Tel: 773-549-5538.
Bringing together the cuisines of Mexico and Ecuador, this tiny restaurant specializes in fried pork, goat stew and favourites like tacos and tostadas. $

[O] ANNA MARIA PASTERIA,
4400 North Clark Street;
Tel: 773-506-2662.
Traditional southern Italian food is on the menu, and the deserts are quite good. $$

granite engraved with Van der Rohe's name and the dates of his birth and death.

9 Walk south on Lake Avenue for about 10 paces as it bends into Center Avenue. Continue south on Center Avenue for 15 paces or so as it filters into Main Avenue. Turn right onto Main Avenue and walk west for about 15 paces to the cemetery entrance. As you pass through the cemetery gates go west across North Clark Street to the CTA bus stop.

Albany Park: An Ethnic Mosaic in Chicago Style

Get a sense of the history of this ethnically diverse neighbourhood as you pass interesting buildings, North Park University campus and public art.

Like many communities on the city's North Side, Albany Park started life as a speculative real estate venture in the late 19th century. When the elevated train arrived in 1907, the community began to grow exponentially, and the area became predominantly Jewish. For the past 30 years, the community has served as a port of entry for immigrants from all around the world. A glance at the signs in the shops along Kedzie and Lawrence avenues will give a sense of the vast linguistic and cultural diversity that can be found in this bustling community. Further on, the 'Big Red' apartment complex is a bit quiet now, but during its heyday it held a motley and ethnically diverse group of recent arrivals that were trying to catch a small piece of the American dream. The North Park University campus offers an interesting counterpoint to the rest of Albany Park as its manicured grounds and talk of textbook knowledge seem to sit squarely outside the chaotic messiness of the surrounding area.

After leaving the CTA Kedzie station, walk east to the platform exit that leads to North Kedzie Avenue. Turn north onto Kedzie Avenue and walk two blocks north to its intersection with West Lawrence Avenue.

You've probably noticed along your CTA trip that the train runs at ground level through this part of the city; it makes for a bit of a surreal experience as you can see directly into the backs of people's homes and into their private lives. As you walk north along Kedzie Avenue, take in all the ethnic bakeries, stores and restaurants. Don't be shy about going in and saying hello, as people are quite friendly in these parts.

2 Turn right onto West Lawrence Avenue and walk one block east to North Albany Avenue. Turn left onto North Albany Avenue and walk two blocks north to the northwest corner of North Albany Avenue and West Gunnison Street.

The massive red apartment building here has changed greatly in the past decade, but in the 1980s and 1990s it was the subject of a fascinating study that really speaks to the ethnic and cultural diversity of Albany Park. Dubbed 'Big Red' by researcher and ethnographer Dwight Conquergood (1949–2004), the building contained a typical Albany Park mix of Cambodians, Thais, African-Americans and others who were striving to make their way in the rough-and-tumble world of Chicago. Conquergood came and

WHERE TO EAT

🍽 PUPUSERIA LAS DELICIAS,
3300 West Montrose Avenue;
Tel: 773-267-5346.
A great place to sample cuisine from El Salvador, Honduras and Guatemala. $

🍽 NOON O' KABAB,
4661 North Kedzie Avenue;
Tel: 773-279-9309.
This small Persian restaurant specializes in beef kebabs cooked over an open fire. $$

🍽 BRASA ROJA,
3125 West Montrose Avenue;
Tel: 773-866-2252.
A Columbian meat-lover's paradise with everything from grilled steaks to rabbit. $$

lived among them, and later wrote up his findings—it's neat to walk by and think about all the interesting interactions that have taken place in this building.

3 Continue walking north on North Albany for two blocks until you come to its intersection with West Carmen Avenue.

Only one park can claim to contain two branches of the Chicago River, and it happens to be Ronan Park. The 13 acres (5.3ha) started life as a small area designated for a pumping station in 1929. Over the decades, the park grew and

169

DISTANCE **2.75 miles (4.42km)**

ALLOW **2.5 hours**

START **CTA train station on North Kedzie Avenue**

FINISH **CTA train station on North Kedzie Avenue**

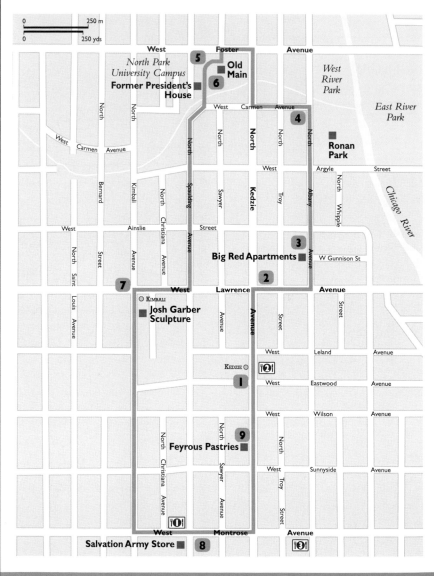

OPPOSITE: PRAIRIE FLOWERS GROW IN THE FRONT YARD OF A RAVENSWOOD MANOR HOME

grew and today you can wander along the path by the river or just sit and enjoy the peace and quiet.

4 Turn left onto West Carmen Avenue and walk two blocks west to the intersection with North Kedzie Avenue. Turn right onto Kedzie Avenue and walk one block north (crossing over the Chicago River) to the intersection with West Foster Avenue, and then turn left on West Foster Avenue and walk one block west to the intersection with North Sawyer Avenue. Continue left for about 10 paces and enter the North Park University campus.

This is what the majority of people think of when they think 'college'. An old Georgian revival building with its gracious columns and multicoloured brick, the 'Old Main' was built in 1894. Look up towards the cupola, which happened to be a landmark for pilots in the 1920s and 1930s who were looking for Orchard Field, known now as O'Hare International Airport.

5 Walk around to the back of the 'Old Main' and follow the path that curves to the left for 10 paces.

This two-storey brick building was the residence of North Park University's President from 1924 to 1958 and it now serves as a one-stop destination for students looking for information about financial aid and other day-to-day activities. It's a tidy house that harks back to the days when a university

president desired to be in close proximity to his (or her) charges.

6 Continue walking along the path in front of the Former President's House until you reach another path that runs in front of the Chicago River. Turn right onto this path and walk 15 paces to a footbridge that crosses the river. After crossing the river you'll be on North Spaulding Avenue. Walk three blocks south on Spaulding Avenue to the intersection with West Lawrence Avenue. Turn right and walk on the south side of West Lawrence Avenue one block to the CTA train station at North Kedzie Avenue.

The station is unremarkable, but the public art here has set off a firestorm of controversy. Created by local artist Josh Garber (born 1963), the 10ft (3m) high aluminium sculpture appears to resemble a tulip, and you can sit on it. Some residents suggested it resembled a certain part of the male anatomy, and asked that it be modified. Garber and community leaders who approved the project stuck to their guns, and it remains here for visitors to judge for themselves.

7 At North Kimball Avenue, turn left and walk south four blocks to the intersection with West Montrose Avenue. Turn left onto West Montrose Avenue and walk along the south side of the street for two blocks to the Salvation Army store at the southwest corner of North Spaulding Avenue and West Montrose Avenue.

You may ask 'What am I doing in this thrift store?' but this is one of the best ways to get a feel for the cultural milieu of Albany Park. In one corner there may be a Guatemalan woman and her kids shopping for clothes, and in another there might be a Turkish man looking at the hardly used television sets. It's a fun place to wander around in, even if you don't need an old macramé wall hanging.

8 After leaving the thrift store, continue walking east on West Montrose Avenue for two blocks to North Kedzie Avenue. Turn left (staying on the west side of Kedzie) and walk north on Kedzie for one block to the intersection with West Sunnyside Avenue. Cross north over West Sunnyside Avenue and five paces later you'll be in front of Feyrous Pastries at 4510 North Kedzie Avenue.

In some ways, Feyrous is like many typical Middle East groceries and bakeries in Albany Park. There's a pile of random Middle Eastern items in one corner, a generous supply of *fava* beans, and a whole range of baked goods (truly the specialty here); the butter cookies and *baklava* are excellent.

9 Continue walking north for one and half blocks to return to the CTA train station on North Kedzie Avenue.

SIGNS IN KOREAN ILLUSTRATE THE EXTENT OF THE ETHNIC MIX LIVING IN ALBANY PARK

INDEX

ACKNOWLEDGEMENTS

The Automobile Association would like to thank the following photographers, companies and picture libraries for their assistance in the preparation of this book. Abbreviations for the picture credits are as follows: (AA) AA World Travel Library.

Front cover: AA/S M Taylor; 3 AA/C Sawyer; 7 AA/S M Taylor; 8 Photolibrary Group; 11 © Thomas A. Heinz/Corbis; 13 Max Grinnell; 14 © Chicagoview/Alamy; 17 © Kim Karpeles/Alamy; 18 AA/C Sawyer; 19/20 © Kim Karpeles/Axiom; 22 © Sandy Felsenthal/Corbis; 25 Andrew Leyerles/Dorling Kindersley/Getty Images; 27 AA/P Wood; 28 © Art on File/Corbis; 29 © Kim Karpeles/Alamy; 31 © Kim Karpeles/Alamy; 32 AA/S M Taylor; 34/35 © Richard Cummins/Corbis; 36 Tim Boyle/Getty Images; 39 Photolibrary Group; 40 AA/C Sawyer; 41 Peter Pearson/Stone/Getty Images; 42/43 © Richard Cummins/Corbis; 44 © Kevin Fleming/Corbis; 45 Photolibrary Group; 47 AA/P Wood; 48 © Ralf-Finn Hestoft/Corbis; 50 AA/P Wood; 51 AA/P Wood; 53 © Chicagoview/Alamy; 55 © Daniella Delimont/ Alamy; 56 AA/C Sawyer; 59 AA/C Sawyer; 60/61 AA/C Sawyer; 62/63 AA/C Sawyer; 64 © Kim Karpeles/Alamy; 65 © Michele Falzone/ Alamy; 67 © chicagoview/Alamy; 68 © Kim Karpeles/Alamy; 70 © Marion Kaplan/Alamy; 73 © Marion Kaplan/Alamy; 75 AA/P Wood; 76/77 © Andre Jenny/Alamy; 78 © Sandy Felsenthal/Corbis; 81 © Alen MacWeeney/Corbis; 82/83 Michael L Abramson/Time Life Pictures/Getty Images; 84 AA/P Wood; 85 AA/C Sawyer; 87 AA/C Sawyer; 88 AA/P Wood; 90/91 AA/C Sawyer; 92 © EDIFICE/Alamy; 95 Matt Carmichael/Getty Images; 96/97 © Danita Delimont/Alamy; 98 © Kim Karpeles/Alamy; 101 © Kim Karpeles/Alamy; 102 © Kim Karpeles/Alamy; 103 Tim Boyle/Getty Images; 104/105 AA/C Sawyer; 106 AA/C Sawyer; 107 Max Grinnell; 109 © Kim Karpeles/Alamy; 110 Andrew Leyerle/Dorling Kindersley/Getty Images; 112 © Kim Karpeles/Alamy; 115 Photolibrary Group; 116 © Louis K. Meisel Gallery, Inc./Corbis; 118/119 © Alen MacWeeney/Corbis; 120 © Art on File/Corbis; 122/123 © Arcaid/Corbis; 126 Photolibrary Group; 129 MPI/Stringer/Hulton Archive/Getty Images; 131 © Thomas A. Heinz/Corbis; 132/133 © Kelly-Mooney Photography/Corbis; 134 © Linda Matlow/Alamy; 137 © Mathias Beinling/Alamy; 138 © Sandy Felsenthal/Corbis; 140/141 Karina Wang/Photographer's Choice/Getty Images; 142 © Sandy Felsenthal/Corbis; 145 Wayne C. Toberman/fotolibra; 146 © Sandy Felsenthal/Corbis; 147 Wayne C. Toberman/fotolibra; 148 © Kim Karpeles/Alamy; 149 © Kim Karpeles/Axiom; 151 © Linda Matlow/Alamy; 152 © Sarah Hadley/Alamy; 154 © Bettmann/Corbis; 155 © Richard Cummins/Corbis; 156 © Kelly-Mooney Photography/Corbis; 158/159 Photolibrary Group; 160 Photolibrary Group; 161 Photolibrary Group; 162 Wayne C. Toberman/fotolibra; 163 © Andrew Woodley/Alamy; 165 Wayne C. Toberman/fotolibra; 166/167 © Art on File/Corbis; 168 © Kim Karpeles/Alamy; 171 © Kim Karpeles/Alamy; 172/173 © Kim Karpeles/Alamy.

Every effort has been made to trace the copyright holders, and we apologize in advance for any accidental errors. We would be happy to apply the corrections in the following edition of this publication.